Synkrētic

The Journal of Indo-Pacific
Philosophy, Literature & Cultures

2024 / №5

Synkrētic
The Journal of Indo-Pacific Philosophy, Literature & Cultures
ISSN 2653-4029
Editor: Christian Romuss

www.synkretic.com

General enquiries: enquiries@synkretic.com

Correspondence should be addressed to

The Editor, Synkrētic Journal
c/o Irukandji Media Pty Ltd
Unit 9 204 Alice St
Brisbane City Qld 4000
AUSTRALIA

Synkrētic acknowledges the traditional custodians of the lands of Brisbane on which we work, the Turrbal and Jagera peoples.

Published in Australia by Irukandji Press, Brisbane.

Irukandji Press is a trade name of Irukandji Media Pty Ltd.

ISBN 978-0-6454980-4-2

Layout and editorial matter: © Irukandji Media Pty Ltd, 2024

Essays, responses, stories and notes: © retained by respective authors or their estates and (re)printed here with permission OR source is in the public domain.

The moral rights of the authors have been asserted.

All rights reserved. No part of this publication may be reproduced, stored in a retrieval system, or transmitted in any form by any means without the prior permission in writing of the Editor of Synkrētic.

Cover design and typesetting: Arthur Arek

Contributors

Ruth Aarker · Reverend Dr John · Hayden Kee
Alexandre Kojève · Fritz Mauthner · Christian Romuss
Edward Sapir · Carl Strehlow · Trần Đức Thảo
Edward Burnett Tylor

Acknowledgments

Synkrētic №5 (Jul. 2024) was a collaborative enterprise involving 10 past and current writers.

Contributors to this issue were based in Australia (3), France (1), Germany (1), Hong Kong (1), India (1), the United Kingdom (1), the United States (1), and Vietnam (1).

Synkrētic warmly thanks all rights holders from around the world whose support made this issue possible.

Contents

The word and the world   1

Trần Đức Thảo and *Alexandre Kojève*
Correspondence   5
    TRANSLATED WITH AN INTRODUCTION BY *Hayden Kee*

Carl Strehlow
Myths, sagas, and tales of the Aranda   19
    TRANSLATED BY *Christian Romuss*

Edward Sapir
The meaning of religion   31

Edward Burnett Tylor
Animism   46

Reverend Dr John
The life and writings of Avyar   68

Fritz Mauthner
The critique of language   87
    TRANSLATED BY *Christian Romuss*

Ruth Aarker
Logomania   97

EDITORIAL

The word and the world

Synkrētic was conceived as a home for reflection on the Indo-Pacific's philosophies, literatures, and cultures. That process is carried on not only in the minds of living thinkers and writers, but also in the pages of books once deemed pinnacles of knowledge, now become mere artefacts of the endless quest for insight into the world and ourselves. These records of past theorising on cross-cultural encounter must be read anew by each generation, there can be no final reckoning, no conclusion to a process which lives in the pursuit. No man ever steps in the same river twice, and no man ever opens the same book twice. Yet how easily we render judgment on 'the past' and call bygone eras which, from another standpoint, are contemporary with our own. For every past lives only in the here and now, in the thinking—not the thought—of those who, wandering through the cultural graveyard, are determined to give an account of it, if only to themselves.

In this spirit, *Synkrētic* № 5 proffers to its readers' contemplation several historical texts, some in new translation.

Opening the issue is an exchange of letters between the Vietnamese philosopher Trần Đức Thảo and French philosopher Alexandre Kojève. The correspondence, which centres on the philosophers' divergent readings and appropriations of Hegel, was set in motion by Trần's review in *Les Temps Modernes* of Kojève's lectures on the *Phenomenology of Spirit*. As translator Hayden Kee explains in his introduction, this brief exchange affords us a glimpse into the 'ardent and precocious mind' of Trần, who for reasons of history and nationality knew a different fate from and has not enjoyed the same reputation as his contemporaries Sartre, de Beauvoir, and Merleau-Ponty.

The word and the world

In new translation, extracts from Carl Strehlow's *Myths, Sagas, and Tales of the Aranda* tell of the eternal, emu-footed Altjira whose abode is the sky, and of the *rella manerinja* or 'fused men' who lived on the side of the mountain Erálera. In considering these blackfellastories retold in whitefellatongues, we must ask ourselves to what extent the cultural and professional background of Strehlow, a German Lutheran missionary, informed and shaped this work, even while we must doubt the integrity of whatever answers we propose. For if what we know of the Aranda and their thought-life has come to us through 'our' own intellectual equipment, how do we correct for the distortion of those instruments? How do we find 'the true Aranda' from which to reckon our deviations? And do we not already kid ourselves by supposing an homogenous culture on that side of the encounter—and this?

Edward Sapir, anthropologist and linguist, reflects on the meaning of religion, which he locates not in the formal institution of a church or authoritative scripture but in 'man's never-ceasing attempt to discover a road to spiritual serenity across the perplexities and dangers of daily life.' In Sapir's day, this definition, which sees religion as rooted in the soil of human feeling and behaviour, did justice to the widespread recognition of its ubiquity across cultures; not just 'the more sophisticated peoples' but also 'primitive and barbaric folk' had religion, because they each in their own way sought to turn 'omnipresent fear and a vast humility paradoxically ... into bedrock security.' Sapir's definition still has value in our own day, when under motley banners many who confound atheism with irreligiosity cleave to new pieties in pursuit of the old mission to turn dissenting heathens into bleating denizens of their flock.

In his discussion, Sapir references Edward Burnett Tylor's attempt to trace all forms of religiosity back to animism, and we have reproduced in this issue a selection from the relevant work. The reader who can think her way past (ahistorical) indignation at Tylor's vocabulary will find in the text cultural reports which, in their own right, continue to fascinate. She may also discern a still commendable motive to reckon with cultural differences in a framework of common humanity, even if she cannot endorse an account which ranks cultures by an intuitive and self-serving standard of progress as high or low in 'the scale of humanity'.

From the *Asiatic Researches* comes an account of the life and teachings of Avyar, a Tamil philosopher whose 'origin and birth, as well as the era in which she flourished, are lost in fable' and whose teachings here take the form of precepts timeless in their simplicity.

Fritz Mauthner, through an analysis of the concepts of 'Primitive Philosophy' and 'Religion', reminds us of language's instability and inconsistency across time and place. Salient in the context of Tylor's contribution is Mauthner's remark regarding Wilhelm Wundt's essay 'The Origins of Philosophy and the Philosophy of the Primitive Races', that he 'espouses that dangerous principle of historical scholarship which equates, on one hand, the beginnings of a cultural domain and, on the other, the relevant circumstances of the so-called primitive races of the present day.' In his *Dictionary of Philosophy*, from which his contribution to this issue has been drawn, Mauthner catalogues the word-trove of philosophy and shows it to be filled with what Hobbes before him deemed 'wise men's counters' but 'the money of fools'. Mauthner's skepticism of language perhaps grew too extreme, but his disenchanting reflections on it—which piqued the interest of Beckett, Joyce, and Wittgenstein—are salutary in a species prone to mistaking words for the world.

The ghost of Mauthner animates the concluding contribution from Australian poet Ruth Aarker. Short but cogent, *Logomania* warns against the perils of theory, how words too often serve our selfish ends, and reminds us that, difficult though it may be to locate, there is yet a distinction between the world and what we write, think, and say about it.

Christian Romuss

Correspondence*

Trần Đức Thảo and *Alexandre Kojève*

TRANSLATED WITH AN INTRODUCTION BY
Hayden Kee†

Introduction

Trần Đức Thảo was one of the most remarkable and enigmatic protagonists in the history of 20th century European philosophy. Born on September 26, 1917, near Hanoi in modern-day Vietnam (then the capital of colonial French Indochina), Trần moved to Paris, France in 1936 to study philosophy, attending the prestigious École Normale Supérieure and Sorbonne. He joined there that much celebrated cohort of post-war French intellectuals, including Jean-Paul Sartre, Simone de Beauvoir, and Maurice Merleau-Ponty. Along with Merleau-Ponty, he was one of the first visitors to the newly founded Husserl Archives in Leuven, Belgium during the war, and played a central role in the first efforts to establish a second archive in Paris. Trần and Sartre even attempted to co-author a book, though the collaboration apparently ended acrimoniously. And while Sartre and company would rise to academic and popular celebrity, a different fate was in store for Trần, in large part due to

---

* This is a translation of correspondence originally published in the journal *Genèses* 2 (1990): 131-7.
† Hayden Kee is Assistant Professor in the Department of Philosophy at the Chinese University of Hong Kong. He holds a PhD in philosophy from Fordham University (USA). His research focuses on questions of mind, language, and cognitive science.

his political activism and commitment to Vietnamese independence. That fate was foreshadowed on October 29, 1945, just weeks after the end of World War II, when Sartre delivered his famous 'Existentialism is a Humanism' to a full house of intellectuals and socialites. Meanwhile, Trần sat in a Paris prison cell, detained on charges of threatening French national security because he had been agitating for the independence of Vietnam.

During the war, what remained of French colonial rule in Indochina under Vichy France was undermined by the invasion of the Japanese military. With the capitulation of Japan at the end of the war, the Vietnamese communists under the leadership of Ho Chi Minh seized power and declared Vietnamese independence. The principal victors of the global war, however, did not acknowledge the declaration, and France began planning to reclaim its colony. While in prison, Trần penned 'On Indochina'[1], which was published in early 1946 in Sartre's and Merleau-Ponty's fledgling journal *Les Temps Modernes*. The essay presented an existential-phenomenological analysis of the misunderstanding between coloniser and colonised in Indochina and made a plea to the French people to leave Vietnam in peace. The plea was not heeded, however. French forces returned to Vietnam shortly thereafter, inaugurating decades of bloodshed. 'On Indochina' and Trần's other contributions as *Les Temps Modernes*' Indochina correspondent are perhaps the first instance of a decolonial application of phenomenology. These writings would influence later, better known decolonial authors such as Frantz Fanon and Aimé Césaire.

Trần's primary philosophical concern in the postwar years, as with others in his milieu, was with the relation between the two dominant philosophical movements of the era, Hegelianism-Marxism and existential phenomenology. Trần developed his ideas on this relation in a series of articles published from 1946-1950[2], culminating in his magnum opus, *Phenomenology and Dialectical Materialism*[3], published in 1951. Trần argued that phenomenology was essentially incomplete and that it required the kind of foundation that only Marxist dialectical materialism could provide. Trần's conviction was not only theoretical, but also practical and concretely political. Following the publication of his book, Trần returned in 1951 to a Vietnam still in the midst of its Anti-French Resistance War. He voluntarily undertook 'rectification' training before returning to academic work, publishing in his native language on Vietnamese history and literature. In 1956 he was appointed head of the faculty of history at the national university. However, his views on political liberalisation and his critique of the regime ensnared him in a reactionary political backlash and purge of intellectuals. He was banned from teaching and effectively silenced on political matters. He later returned to philosophical work of a less political nature, resulting in a second book, on the origins of language.[4] Trần returned to Paris in 1991, under somewhat mysterious circumstances[5], and passed away there in 1993. Trần's name was cleared and his legacy restored posthumously in his native Vietnam in 2001 when the party awarded him the Ho Chi Minh Prize, one of the highest prizes the nation grants to its citizens.[6]

It was in the context of those heady post-war years in Paris that Trần entered a brief correspondence with another of the most influential thinkers of the time, Alexandre Kojève. Kojève's lectures on Hegel's *Phenomenology of Spirit* from the 1930s at the École Pratique des Hautes Études decisively shaped the mid-century French reception of Hegel. They were published in 1947 by Gallimard[7], and Trần published a lengthy review discussion of the work in *Les Temps Modernes* in 1948.[8] Trần praised the originality and fecundity of Kojève's interpretation, even hailing it as 'a remarkable moment in the development of Absolute Spirit' (110). But he accused Kojève of overemphasising the importance of the *Phenomenology*'s master-slave dialectic and misunderstanding the nature of Hegelian dialectic. The result, according to Trần, is that Kojève accused Hegel mistakenly of an untenable monism (while Kojève himself regressed into dualism), failed to see the enduring significance of nature in history and freedom, and left the door open for a theistic reappropriation of Hegelian thought. Trần proposed an interpretation of the *Phenomenology* meant to rectify these misunderstandings, albeit one that exhibits Trần's own Marxist-materialist preferences. The mostly friendly discussion between Kojève and Trần was continued in the exchange of letters from October 1948, presented here in translation (with the kind permission of the editors of *Genèses*, where it was published in French in 1990[9]). This slightly more personal medium allows us an alternative glimpse into an ardent and precocious mind whose talents sadly never came fully to fruition due to the vagaries of a cruel and arbitrary century.

Further reading

There are two excellent, short introductions in English to Trần Đức Thảo's life and work, one by Nicolas de Warren[10] and one by Russell Ford.[11] Readers of French will find further details in the collection of essays prepended to the 2013 re-edition of *Phénoménologie et matérialisme dialectique*[12] and in Alexandre Feron's recent study.[13]

Synkrētic

Kojève to Trần

Paris, 7 October 1948

Dear Sir,

I just read your article in *Les Temps Modernes* on *The Phenomenology of Spirit*, which interested me very much. I would first like to thank you for the kind words you saw fit to write about me. I appreciate them all the more, since I continue to feel remorse for letting my book be published in its chaotic state, with which you are familiar.

As to the essentials of the question, I am, on the whole, in agreement with the interpretation of the *Phenomenology* that you give. I would like to point out, however, that my work did not have the character of a historical study. It mattered relatively little to me what Hegel himself wanted to say in his book. I offered a course in phenomenological anthropology, making use of Hegelian texts but saying only what I considered to be the truth and dropping whatever in Hegel seemed to me to be an error. Thus, for example, by renouncing Hegelian monism, I consciously distanced myself from this great philosopher. Furthermore, my course was essentially a work of propaganda intended to shake people's minds. That is why I consciously enhanced the role of the dialectic of Master and Slave and, in a general way, schematised the content of the *Phenomenology*.

This is why I personally believe that it would be highly desirable for you to develop, in the form of a complete commentary, the main lines of interpretation that you have outlined in the article to which I refer.

Just one brief remark: The terms 'sense of self' and 'self-consciousness' are from Hegel himself, who expressly says that, in contrast to man, the animal never goes beyond the stage of 'sense of self.' The term 'struggle of pure prestige' is indeed not found in Hegel, but I believe that this is only a matter of a difference in terminology, for everything I say about this struggle applies perfectly to what Hegel calls the 'struggle for recognition.' Finally, as far as my theory of the 'desire for desire' is concerned, it is not in Hegel either and I am not sure that he saw the matter clearly. I introduced this notion because I intended to make not a commentary on the *Phenomenology*, but an interpretation. In other words, I tried to find the deep premises of the Hegelian doctrine and to construct it by deducing it logically from these premises. The 'desire for desire' seems to me to be one of the fundamental premises in question, and if Hegel himself did not clearly identify it, I believe that, by formulating it explicitly, I have made a certain philosophical progress. This is perhaps the only philosophical progress that I have made, the rest being more or less only philology, which is to say, precisely an explication of texts or a commentary (my 'attack' on 'monism' being nothing but a program).

The most important point is the question of dualism and atheism which you mention in the last section of your article (pp. 517-519). I must say that I do not agree

Synkrētic

with what you say there, but I believe that the divergence is only based on a misunderstanding.

Your reasoning would certainly be correct if it referred to a dualism properly so called, that is to say, an abstract dualism and not a dialectical one. I would say like you that all dualism is necessarily deist, since, if there are two types of Being (Nature and Man), there is necessarily the unity of the two which is, in some way, 'superior' to them, and this unity cannot be conceived other than as a divine entity. But the dualism I have in view is dialectical. Indeed, I used the image of a gold ring, which would not exist as a ring if there were no hole. One cannot say, however, that the hole exists in the same way as gold and that there are here two modes of being, of which the ring is the unity. In our case, the gold is Nature, the hole is Man, and the ring—Spirit. This means that if Nature can exist without Man, and has, in the past, existed without Man, Man has never existed and cannot exist without Nature and outside of it, just as gold can exist without the hole, while the hole simply does not exist if there is no metal around it. Given that Man created himself only in and by, or, more exactly still, as the negation of Nature, it follows that he presupposes Nature. This essentially distinguishes him from all that is divine. Given that he is the negation of nature, he is something other than the divine pagan that is Nature itself; and given that he is the negation of Nature, which, like all negation, presupposes what is negated, he presupposes (ontologically and dialectically) this Nature and is thus different from the Christian God who, on the contrary, is prior to Nature and creates it by a positive act of his will.

I thus do not say that there are simultaneously two modes of being: Nature and Man. I say that until the appearance of the first Man (who was created in a struggle of prestige), Being in its entirety was nothing but Nature. From the moment when Man exists, Being in its entirety is Spirit, since Spirit is nothing other than this very Nature that henceforth implies Man, and from the moment when the real world in fact implies Man, Nature in the strict sense of the word (*i.e.*, the real world minus Man) is nothing but an abstraction. So, until a certain moment in time, there was only Nature and from a certain moment, there is only Spirit. Now, since what is truly real in Spirit (the gold of the ring) is Nature (Man being nothing but the (real, *i.e.*, active) negation of Nature), we can say, as you do, that Spirit is the result of the evolution of Nature itself (this all the more since before the appearance of Man, Nature alone really existed). However, I do not like this way of speaking, because it can lead one to believe that the appearance of Man can be deduced *a priori*, like any other natural event. However, I believe that this is not the case and that if the whole of natural evolution can, in principle, be deduced *a priori*, the appearance of Man and his history can only be deduced *a posteriori*, that is to say, precisely, not deduced or foreseen, but only understood. This is a way of saying that the act of self-creation of Man remains an act of freedom and that the whole series of human acts which constitute history is itself a series of free acts. This is why I prefer to

Synkrētic

speak of a dualism between Nature and Man, but it would be more correct to speak of a dualism between Nature and Spirit, Spirit being that very Nature that implies Man. My dualism is thus not 'spatial,' but 'temporal': Nature first, then Spirit or Man. There is a dualism because Spirit or Man cannot be deduced from Nature, the break being made by the act of creative freedom of Nature, that is to say, the act of negating freedom of Nature.

I would be very grateful to you, Dear Sir, if you could tell me in a few words to what extent the explanations (admittedly very insufficient) that I provide you in this letter may reply to the objections that you have made to me.

Sincerely, Dear Sir, with all my sympathy,

A. Kojève

Trần to Kojève

Paris, 30 October 1948

Dear Sir,

I have just received your letter and thank you very much for the clarifications you have given me. They agree, moreover, with what I myself think, since, as you may have noticed, I read your book with the greatest sympathy. I simply believe that you are not going far enough and that by refusing to draw the materialist conclusions of atheistic humanism, you are leaving room, without realising it, for a return to religious humanism. If space had not been limited, and if I had not first had to focus on the essentials of the question, I would have insisted [in my article] even more on the considerable progress you have made on the conventional interpretations of Hegel. But since you think that the domain of the spirit is essentially historical, you cannot be surprised that your doctrine, which might have seemed revolutionary ten or so years ago, is no longer so after the events that have since upset the course of the world and given it a completely new figure.

Naturally, it is not a question here of some mediocre problem of erudition, and one could not criticise a work like yours on the few divergences which may arise with Hegel's text. I have only mentioned them for the record and in passing. It was also necessary to note your originality, which the ordinary reader may have failed to recognise.

I must, however, reiterate in this connection that I never denied the existence in Hegel of the distinction between 'self-consciousness' and 'sense of self,' and I would ask you to believe that I was not ignorant of the relevant texts. I simply remarked, if you would read me carefully, that it [*i.e.*, the distinction] is not found in the passage in question (Chapter IV), where it obviously could play no role, since at stake in this place is removing abstract oppositions and engendering the human from the animal.

As for the 'struggle of pure prestige,' it is presented, in the definition you give of it, as an immediate and unconditioned negation of natural existence. But a concept of this kind can find no place in Hegel, where negation is always mediated. In the case that concerns us, it can only arise as the result of that of which it is a negation, namely the nature which negates itself by affirming itself. The struggle of self-consciousnesses begins on the animal level and is completed, through the internal logic of its movement, on the human level.

On this subject, it would be very difficult for me to accept the reconciliation that you propose, where, taking up Kant's distinction between *folgen* and *erfolgen*, you consent to say that spirit is the result of the becoming of nature, specifying that it is an absolutely contingent event and not a necessary consequence. However, you know very well that in Hegel the result derives from its principle in a movement whose necessity is identical with freedom. Of course, this is a dialectical movement, which excludes any *a priori* deduction. It can only be understood historically or posited in a praxis. But comprehension and action here imply an intelligibility, which is precisely denied in your doctrine of freedom.

I have of course never attributed a crudely 'spatial' dualism to you. But I do not believe it's possible to transform the dialectical passage from nature to spirit into a pure, contingent succession based on a totally arbitrary act of negation. For Hegel, negation is identical to affirmation and does nothing but realise it in its true being. If there is indeed duality, then this duality is identical to unity. And it is not at all a question of mind games: I have precisely tried to show how materialist Marxism makes it possible to give real content to these fundamental dialectical notions.

Hence, I don't reproach you for having separated nature and spirit, but rather for not having recognised that this separation only realises their identity. For it follows that the separation can only be explained by a divine transcendence. Naturally, you reject this consequence, since you define freedom by the exclusion of all intelligibility of whatever kind. But man can renounce understanding the reason of things. And because you refuse to find the motive of separation in unity itself, the theologian will conclude that it derives from an incarnation.

But perhaps we do not belong to the same family of spirits. For before tackling contemporary philosophy, I was a convinced Spinozist, and I know that this is a doctrine that you hardly appreciate. You define freedom by the negation of necessity. I defend the great rationalist tradition which has always identified them.

Sincerely, Dear Sir, with my best wishes,

Thao

Notes

1 Trần Đức Thảo, "Sur l'Indochine," *Les Temps Modernes* vol. 1, no. 5 (February 1946): 878–900; English translation Trần Đức Thảo, "On Indochina," ed. and trans. Hayden Kee, *Études Phénoménologiques - Phenomenological Studies* vol. 5 (2021): 1–24.
2 Trần Đức Thảo, "Marxisme et Phénoménologie," *Revue Internationale*, no. 2 (1946): 168–74; English translation Trần Đức Thảo, "Marxism and Phenomenology," trans. Nicolas de Warren, *Graduate Faculty Philosophy Journal* vol. 30, no. 2 (October 1, 2009): 327–35; Trần Đức Thảo, "La Phénoménologie de l'esprit et Son Contenu Réel," *Les Temps Modernes* vol. 3, no. 36 (1948): 492–519; English translation Trần Đức Thảo, "The Phenomenology of Mind and Its Real Content," *Telos*, no. 8 (1971): 91–110; Trần Đức Thảo, "Existentialisme et Matérialisme Dialectique," *Revue de Métaphysique et de Morale* vol. 54, no. 3/4 (1949): 317–29; English translation Trần Đức Thảo, "Existentialism and Dialectical Materialism," trans. Nicolas de Warren, *Graduate Faculty Philosophy Journal* vol. 30, no. 2 (October 1, 2009): 285–95; Trần Đức Thảo, "Les Origines de La Réduction Phénoménologique Chez Husserl," *Deucalion* vol. 58, no. 3 (1950): 128–42; English translation Trần Đức Thảo, "The Origins of the Phenomenological Reduction in Husserl," trans. Nicolas de Warren, *Graduate Faculty Philosophy Journal* vol. 30, no. 2 (October 1, 2009): 337–48.
3 Trần Đức Thảo, *Phénoménologie et Matérialisme Dialectique* (Paris: Éditions Minh Tan, 1951); English translation Trần Đức Thảo, *Phenomenology and Dialectical Materialism*, trans. Daniel J. Herman and Donald V. Morano (Dordrecht: Springer, 1986).
4 Trần Đức Thảo, *Recherches Sur l'origine Du Langage et de La Conscience* (Paris: Éditions sociales, 1973); English translation Trần Đức Thảo, *Investigations into the Origins of Language and Consciousness*, trans. Daniel J. Herman and Robert L. Armstrong (Dordrecht: Springer, 1984).
5 See Thierry Marchaisse, "Tombeau sur la mort de Tran Duc Thao," in *L'itinéraire de Tran Duc Thao: Phénoménologie et transfert culturel*, ed. Jocelyn Benoist and Michel Espagne (Paris: Colin, 2013).
6 Shawn McHale, "Vietnamese Marxism, Dissent, and the Politics of Postcolonial Memory: Tran Duc Thao, 1946-1993," *The Journal of Asian Studies* vol. 61, no. 1 (2002): 7–31.
7 Alexandre Kojève, *Introduction à la lecture de Hegel: leçons sur la Phénoménologie de l'Esprit professées de 1933 à 1939 à l'École des Hautes Études*, ed. Raymond Queneau (Paris: Gallimard, 1980); English translation Alexandre Kojève, *Introduction to the Reading of Hegel: Lectures on the "Phenomenology of Spirit,"* ed. Raymond Queneau and Allan Bloom, trans. James H. Nichols, First Edition (Ithaca: Cornell University Press, 1980).
8 Trần, "La Phénoménologie de l'esprit et Son Contenu Réel"; English translation Trần, "The Phenomenology of Mind and Its Real Content."
9 Gwendoline Jarczyk and Pierre-Jean Labarrière, "Alexandre Kojève et Tran-Duc-Thao. Correspondance inédite," *Genèses. Sciences sociales et histoire* vol. 2, no. 1 (1990): 131–37.
10 Nicolas de Warren, "Hopes of a Generation: The Life, Work, and Legacy of Tran Duc Thao," *Graduate Faculty Philosophy Journal* vol. 30, no. 2 (2009): 263–83.

11 Russell Ford, "Tran Duc Thao: Politics and Truth," *Philosophy Compass* 15 (January 1, 2020): e12650.
12 Jocelyn Benoist and Michel Espagne, eds., *L'itinéraire de Tran Duc Thao: Phénoménologie et transfert culturel* (Paris: Colin, 2013).
13 Alexandre Feron, *Le Moment marxiste de la phénoménologie française: Sartre, Merleau-Ponty, Trần Đức Thảo* (Springer, 2021).

Myths, sagas, and tales of the Aranda*

Carl Strehlow†

TRANSLATED BY *Christian Romuss*‡

Altjira

According to the traditions of the ancients there is a highest good (*mara*) being, Altjira. This being is eternal (*ngambakala*)[1] and is represented as a large strong man red of skin, whose long fair hair (*gola*) falls down over his shoulders. Altjira has emu's feet (*ilia* = emu, *inka* = legs, feet) and is therefore called Altjira Iliinka. He is painted with a white stripe on his forehead (*tjilara*), a necklace (*matara*) and an armband (*gultja*), he also wears a belt (*tjipa*) made out of hair, as well

---

* This extract is from Carl Strehlow's *Mythen, Sagen und Märchen des Aranda-Stammes in Zentral-Australien*, the first part of the seven-volume *Die Aranda- und Loritja-Stämme in Zentral-Australien* (Frankfurt: Joseph Brauer & Co, 1907-20). This work is in the public domain in the original German. Two English translations of the complete work are known to exist, but these either have not been published or are not readily available. For this translation, Strehlow's spelling of Aboriginal (Aranda and Loritja) words has been preserved, and these have been italicised unless the translator has understood them to be proper nouns. Except where indicated, endnotes are Strehlow's from the source text. All instances of 'McDonnell Ranges' have been corrected to 'MacDonnell Ranges'.

† Carl Friedrich Theodor Strehlow (1871-1922) was a German-Australian linguist, anthropologist, and Lutheran missionary. In October 1894, he became superintendent of the Finke River Mission at Hermannsburg in the Northern Territory, at that time under the administration of South Australia. He remained in this position until his death.

‡ Christian Romuss is a Brisbane-based translator. He is editor of *Synkrētic*.

as a *worrabakana* [loin cloth]. He has many wives, called *ineera* [the beautiful ones], who have dog's feet (*knulja-inka*) and, like Altjira himself, are red of skin. He has many sons and daughters, of which the former have emu's feet, the latter dog's feet. He is surrounded by beautiful young men and girls.

His abode is the sky (*alkira*), which has existed since eternity (*ngambakala*); this sky the natives imagine as a continent. The milky way is a great river (called *larra*, also *ulbaia* = creek), with high trees and inexhaustible springs of fresh water; here there are fine-tasting berries and fruits in abundance; swarms of birds enliven the great realm of Altjira, while many animals, such as kangaroos (*āra*), wild cats (*tjilpa*), and the like roam his immense hunting grounds. While Altjira himself hunts the game that comes to quench its thirst at the springs, the wives of Altjira gather *latjia* [edible roots with turnip-like leaves], *jelka*[2] and other fruits which grow there in excess in every season of the year. The stars (with the exception of some constellations which are considered totem-gods risen to the sky) are the campfires of Altjira.

Altjira is the good god of the Aranda, who is known not only to the men but also to the women. His dominion, however, extends only over the sky; he neither created men nor do their lives concern him. *Tjurunga*[3]-woods or -stones of Altjira do not exist. The Aranda neither fear Altjira nor do they love him; their only fear is that one day the sky might collapse and kill them all. The sky rests on pillars or, as the Aranda say, on stone legs.

Note: A linguistic derivation of the word *Altjira* has not yet been found; the natives now connect with it the concept of not-having-become; asked about the meaning, they assured me repeatedly that *Altjira* denotes one who has no beginning, who is not produced by another (*erina itja arbmanakala* = him no-one has created). When Spencer and Gillen (*Northern Tribes of Central Australia*) assert: 'the word *alcheri* means dream', this assertion is not accurate. Dreaming is *altjirerama*, derived from *altjira* [God] and *rama* [to see], therefore: 'to see God'. Likewise in the Loritja language to dream = *tukura nangani*, composed out of *tukura* = God and *nangani* = to see. I will show later that, in this regard, the terms *altjira* and *tukura* are not be taken as referring to the highest God of heaven but only a totem-god which the native believes he sees in his dreams. Dream in the

Synkrētic

Aranda language is not *alcheri*, but rather *altjirerinja*, yet this word is seldom used, usually the black man says: *ta altjireraka* = it dreamed to me. The word *alcheringa*, which according to Spencer and Gillen is supposed to mean 'dreamtime', is obviously a corruption of *altjirerinja*. Of a 'dreamtime' as a temporal period, by the way, the native knows nothing; what is meant is the time in which the *Aldjiranga mitjina* wandered the earth.

The Primordial Age

The earth (*āla*), which is likewise eternal (*ngambakala*), was in the beginning covered by the sea (*laia*). Out of this immense mass of water protruded various mountains on which lived individual beings endowed with divine powers, *altjirangamitjina* [the eternal uncreated]; these same beings are also labelled *inkara* [the immortal ones]. In the northern MacDonnell Ranges, for example, there rose up above the surface of the great water a high mountain called Torulba[4], and on this mountain two kangaroo (*aranga*)[5]-men led their lives. Also in the vicinity of the Finke Gorge, at the place where the Finke River breaks through the MacDonnell Ranges, stood a high cliff with the name Erálera [the resolute], on the inside of which there was a great cave in which duck (*wonkara*)-men lived. Since they found on the water-covered earth no nourishment, these *wonkara*-men flew time and again up to the sky in order to hunt in the realm of Altjira and returned laden with quarry to Erálera.

On the side of this mountain (*patta itéela*)[6] there were many unevolved men, called *rella manerinja*[7] because their limbs were fused. Their eyes and ears were closed (*manta*), in place of the mouth there was a small round aperture, their fingers as well as their toes were fused (*manerinja*), their hands clenched in fists had fused to their chests (*turba* or *innopúta*)[8] and their legs were drawn up against their bodies. Furthermore, these helpless beings in human form were fused to each other, for which reason they are also designated *rella intarinja* (fused men). These *rella manerinja* who lived on the side of the mountain were divided in four classes: Purula, Kamara, Ngala and Mbitjana, which—because they lived on dry land—were called *ālarinja*[9] [land-dwellers]. Other unevolved men, however, lived in the water, and for that reason were called *kwatjarinja*,[10] water-dwellers. The latter had long hair and lived on raw meat; they were likewise divided in four classes: Pananka, Platara, Knuraia, and Bangata.[11] Such unevolved men were also located in Rubuntja in the north-east and in Irbmankara (now called Running Waters) on the Finke River. Of other places the local Aranda know nothing.

When, later, Altjira forbade the *altjirangamitjina* to hunt in his realm, an *urbura*[12]-totem-god took hold of a stick (*tnauia*) and with it struck the water and commanded: *Jerrai!*[13] [Be gone!], whereupon the sea (*laia*) in the north receded and dry land appeared. Ignoring Altjira's commandment, some *ingkara*, the *wetoppetoppa* [the snakes] climbed up to the sky to hunt there, whereupon at Altjira's bidding the high mountain Erálera sank into the ground (*ralaka*), such that the way back was cut off for the *wetoppetoppa* and they were compelled to remain up in the sky where they now lead an eternal existence as stars. When the Erálera mountain sank down into the deep, the *rella manerinja*, who had hitherto lived on the mountain's side, settled on the shore of a great waterhole (*intjanga*), while those which found themselves in the water built for themselves a great nest on a small island which lay in the body of water. This body of water is located near the Finke Gorge and is now called Aroalirbaka.[14]

When the water had receded from the land, there arose everywhere out of the earth the *altjirangamitjina* [the eternal uncreated, the totem-gods[15]], which hitherto had dwelt in subterranean caves. These appeared most often in human form, yet they were endowed with superhuman powers and possessed the ability to bring forth those animals whose names they held, hence they can be called totem-gods. They were also able at any moment to metamorphose into the animal forms which they brought forth; many even wandered about permanently as animals, such as, for example, the kangaroo (*āra*), the emu (*ilia*), the eagle (*eritja*), amongst others, which in the relevant traditions are referred to simply as animals. In all totem-gods, the characteristic qualities and idiosyncrasies of the relevant animal come to the fore. The kangaroo totem-god eats grass like a real kangaroo and flees from its pursuers; the emu-men run around in the form of emus, eat inmóta[16] bushes, thorns and coals, yet they can also disappear into the earth and wander on beneath its surface, performing ritual acts, and so on. The duck-*altjirangamitjina*, in contrast, wander in human form from one place to another until they spin for themselves a long thread and, sitting upon it, fly through the air in duck-form. The *ngapa*[17]-man plays in this tradition the role of a thief who is killed for his theft, while the 'mischievous' echidna (*inalanga*) for its sacrilege when the circumcision was carried out is hit with so many spears that its body is entirely covered with spears which turn into spines so that from this time on all echidnas have spines, and so on.

To these totem-gods belong certain places where they lived and brought forth their totem-animals. These places are located for the most part either near a high mountain, a water source, or a rocky gorge where the totem-animals who bear their names can usually be found in larger numbers. Thus a lizard totem-place is located in the vicinity of Hermannsburg near Manángananga,[18] where there are many lizards. A fish totem-place is found only in water-places teeming with fish, *e.g.*, in Ellery Creek. Some of these totem-gods remained in their ancestral abodes; these are called *atua kutata*,[19] *i.e.*, men who always live in one location. Other *altjirangamitjina*, in contrast, made long journeys and later returned with some young men to their home. On these journeys they instructed their novices, performed almost every day cult acts which had the aim of inducting their novices into the secrets of men (and as such these acts are called *intijiuma* [= induct, instruct]) and of effecting the prosperity and multiplication of their totem; in this connection they are called *mbatjalkaljuma* [= to put in a good state, to make fruitful, as for example the rain makes the arid land fruitful].[20] However, in whichever place they lost a *tjurunga*, there arose a tree or a rock from which child-seeds enter into transient women such that all these places where they stopped for a while are seen as small totem-places. Next to those totem-places they killed on these journeys many wild animals and the totem-chief worked wonders with his long stick called *tnatantja*[21], which on his wanderings he carried over his shoulder, cutting a path over steep mountain ranges, and so on.

Myths, sagas, and tales of the Aranda

Utterly exhausted (*borka indóra*)[22] they arrived in their home country[23] where they were expected and called by a totem-god who there dwelt (*raiankama*).[24] This totem-god as well as the arrivals entered a stone cave there located, called *arknanaua*[25], threw themselves on the floor out of tiredness (*iwulama*) and their bodies were turned partly into wood, partly into stone (*altjamaltjerama*),[26] which are called *tjurunga*, i.e., the 'proper, hidden' body.

Other totem-gods, in particular those which remained in the totem-place, went at the conclusion of their earthly activity into the earth with their legs, whereupon their bodies were transformed into trees (*inna*) or into stones (*patta*). The tree into which the body of the totem-god was transformed is called *inna ngarra* [the eternal tree], the stone is called *patta ngarra*[27] [the eternal stone]. Such a tree or stone is not to be harmed. Whoever cuts down or merely damages an *inna ngarra* was, in earlier times, punished with death; an animal or bird which seeks refuge on such a tree may not be killed; not even a bush may be cut down, nor the grass burned off in the immediate vicinity of the tree. The 'eternal stones' too must be handled reverentially; they may be neither moved from their place nor broken into pieces.

The souls of the totem-gods went into the earth, they are called *iwopata*, i.e., those hidden within, the invisible; they are called by the eastern Aranda *erintarinja*. These souls of the totem-gods which have entered into the earth live there dressed in a red body in great subterranean caves and are also called *rella ngantja*[28] [hidden men]; in the night they come forth out of the earth in order to take their earlier bodies, namely the *tjurunga*-woods or -stones, in hand and contemplate them; they also want to kill on the earth *aroa* (wallaby), *tjilpa* (native cats) or *ramaia* (lizard species); the killed game they take with them into their subterranean abode, *ralpara*.[29]

The places where the *altjirangamitjina* metamorphosed into *tjurunga*—i.e., into trees or, as the case may be, stones—are called *mbatjita* [great totem-place], also *tmarutja* [eternal place] or *takuta* [everlasting place]. The camping places, in contrast, where they merely sojourned, where they slept in the course of their journey, are called *takapa* [temporary place to stay]. In the latter places, which are of secondary importance relative to the former, either a totem-ancestor remained behind wearied and was then transformed into an *inna ngarra*, or the wandering totem-god lost a *tjurunga* in the latter location which then sank into the earth and became a *ngarra*-tree or -stone. Generally, with regard to the totem-descendants which there arose, the totem-places are called *knanakala*[30] [arisen of its own accord].

Apart from these totem-gods there lived on the earth in ancient times also many *tnéera* [beautiful women] who commanded supernatural powers; some *tnéera* made the initially blind animals and birds able to see. Also *alknarintja*—i.e., women who were never permitted to marry, but had to avert their eyes (*alkna*) from men—lived in various places of the broad territory of the Aranda; either they stayed permanently at one and the same place (*alknarintja kutata*) or they made long, wearisome journeys. They as well as the *tnéera* were transformed into stones (*patta kalkna*)[31] or shrubs (*rula*), while their souls went into the earth where they now live on as *tnoara* [the hidden ones]; by the Aranda of the east these are called also *kawarkinka*. Whoever damages or destroys such a stone (*patta ngarra*) or shrub (*rula ngarra*) into which one of the mentioned women has metamorphosed must fear her vengeance.

For a long time after the earth had become dry, the *rella manerinja* [fused men] lived on in their helpless state until one Mangarkunjerkunja[32] [fly-catcher], the totem-god of a fly-eating species of lizard, came from the north and improved their lot. With a stone knife (*banga*) he first separated the individual beings from each other (*itjaraka*)[33], cut eyes for them (*alkna itjaraka*), opened their ears (*ilba altjurilaka*)[34], their mouth (*arágata*), and the nose (*ala altjurilaka*), separated the individual fingers (*iltja itjaraka*) and the toes (*inka itjaraka*) from each other and circumcised them (*intunaka*) with a stone knife (*lélara*); he even performed on them the subincision (*araltakaka*). He then showed them how to make fire by friction (*matja womma*) and how they ought to prepare their food in future, gave them spear (*tjatta*), spear-thrower (*ninra*), shield (*alkuta*) and boomerang (*ulbarinja*), and to each a *tjurunga*. He impressed upon them the importance of upholding the ceremony of circumcision. To them he also gave a marriage ordinance which regulated the marriages between the classes. According to his instructions, the two groups which already at the beginning had been precisely distinguished and separated were supposed to marry amongst each other in the following manner:

I. Land-Dwellers		II. Water-Dwellers
Purula	*should marry*	Pananka
Kamara	*should marry*	Paltara
Ngala	*should marry*	Knuraia
Mbitjana	*should marry*	Bangata

and vice versa. Thereafter, Mangarkunjerkunja distributed the vast territory which the Aranda inhabit today amongst the four classes. To the Purula and Kamara he allocated the wide region from Jabalpa,[35] called Finke Gorge by the whites, to Rubula [mixture], since here Ellery Creek from the north mixes with the Finke River. To the Ngala and Mbitjana he gave a smaller, enclosed region, from Rubula up to Manta [secluded place] in the vicinity of Running Waters on the lower Finke, while the Pananka and Bangata received the region from Rubula to Rubuntja[36] [great bushfire] on the upper course of Ellery Creek. To the Paltara and Knuraia he allocated abodes in the region from Manta to Altanta,[37] which the whites in Erldunda have corrupted, far in the south; other Paltara and Knuraia were sent by Mangarkunjerkunja to the east in order to populate the region near Tjoritja, today known as Alice Springs.[38] After he had accomplished his work, he returned to the north; the inhabitants of Kujunba[39] [boys-place] had, when Mangarkunjerkunja was accomplishing his work in the south, migrated to the north, such that Mangarkunjerkunja was unable to circumcise them, hence they are called *ilbmarka* [the uncircumcised]. On the tribes which inhabit the north cost of Australia, too, Mangarkunjerkunja did not perform circumcision because he was already too tired

Synkrētic

(*borka indóra*), for which reason these coastal tribes are not familiar with circumcision and the Aranda call them with contempt *worrangulparra* [boys with foreskins]. Later there came another Mangarkunjerkunja from the north; this Mangarkunjerkunja went farther into the south, as far as Albelta[40] [white creek] near Tunga,[41] called Henbury by the whites, where he brought several *rella manerinja* to perfection. This Mangarkunjerkunja returned to the north after he too had formed the undeveloped men living in the west and had carried out circumcision on them. These two Mangarkunjerkunja are considered the greatest benefactors of the Aranda.

Later, abuses regarding the practice of circumcision began to spread; some omitted to perform it entirely; others, such as the *arkularkua*[42] people, performed circumcisions with burning pieces of gumtree bark called *mearkuméarka*, while the *inalanga-* or echidna-men castrated the youngsters such that almost all boys on whom this ceremony was performed died as a consequence. There came then from Nibata in the north two hawk-men—namely Lákabara [black hawk] and Linjalenga [grey hawk], who first performed this ceremony on each other making use of a stone knife (*lélara*)—to the south and circumcised the people again with a *lélara*; they taught the people the correct performance of this ceremony and impressed upon them the importance of steadfastly upholding this ceremony. If they should omit to perform this rite on a boy, then that boy would become an *erintja* or evil being, who would secretly take away from all men their spears and would heap these up, sticking them into the earth. He would climb up onto this heap in order from there to kill with the spears and consume all the inhabitants of the camping place, men, women, and children.

The ordinance of marriage which the Mangarkunjerkunja had given to men also deterioriated. Particularly amongst the emu-men who lived in the south in Unkatji [sleeping place of the emu (Loritja word)], the most unbridled wilfulness grew rampant, such that a man was even able to marry his *maia*, *i.e.*, mother or sister of the mother, his aunt, the latter being what is here meant; indeed, the father married his own daughter after the death of his wife. This moral corruption spread ever farther into the north until a *tnunka* [rat-kangaroo]-man named Katukankara[43] [the immortal father] set out from Antjatjiringi in the north and once again impressed upon the Aranda the laws of marriage which Mangarkunjerkunja had already given them.

It is a conspicuous trait in the traditions of the Aranda that almost all their benefactors who gave them good laws came from the north, whereas evil had spread out from the south. The *inalanga-* or echidna-man came from the south and the *iliarinja-* or emu-people who lived in the south are likewise described as *kunna* (morally evil).

Notes

1 In the Aranda language, there are four words for eternal – *ngambakala, ngambintja, ngamitjina,* and *ngarra.*
2 *jelka*, the onion-like tubours of the *Cyperus rotundus* L., the main food-source of women.
3 *tjurunga* = *churinga* in Spencer and Gillen.
4 *Torulba* ['cliff top, mountain top'], today called Mt Giles, approx. 4260ft above sea level.
5 *aranga* is the grey kangaroo (*Macropus robustus* [Gould]) which stops on the mountains.
6 *patta* = mountain and *itéela* = beside, on the side, on the slope
7 *manerinja* = fused, grown together, sticking together; *rella* = man (human), men
8 *innopúta* presumably = *inapertwa* in Spencer and Gillen.
9 *āla* = land, earth; the ending *rinja* expresses: dwelling, occupying, belong to something.
10 *kwatja* = water, rain
11 As summarising designations of four classes each, the words *ālarinja* and *katjarinja* are not used today; in contrast, Pmaljanuka (Purula, Kamara, Ngala, Mbitjana) and Lakakia (Pananka, Paltara, Knuraia, Bangata) are customary.
12 *urbura*, a small bird similar to a magpie (*Cracticus nigricularis* [Gould])
13 *jerrai* is an expression borrowed from the Loritja language; it is the imperative form of *jennani* = to go, to go forth.
14 *Aroalirbaka*, from *aroa* = wallaby and *irbaka* = has entered into, because according to tradition at this place a wallaby-totem-man went into the waterhole.
15 The specific *altjirangamitjina* of a person is called *iningukua*; the *altjirangamitjina* of the mother is also called *atjira* for short.
16 *inmóta* (*inmátoa*) is a herb which the emus like to eat, which however is also steamed and eaten by the natives; its flavour is disgusting.

Synkrētic

17 *ngapa* is the black crow (*Corvus coronoides* [Vig. Et Horsf.]).
18 *Manangananga* means: the mother with her two children, she has entered with her two sons the stone cave there.
19 *atua* = man, men, *kulata* = always.
20 Spencer and Gillen are wrong when they describe the latter ceremonies as *intijiuma*; rather, the displays which the young men are shown during the induction ceremonies are called *intijiuma*.
21 *tnatantja* is a long staff wrapped with yarn and stuck with bird-down which during the circumcision ceremonies is shown to the young men. This staff represents the spear of the totem-ancestors. Specer and Gillen call it *nurtunja*.
22 *borka* = tired, *indora* = very
23 'Home' designates the location where the *altjirangamitja* first came forth out of the earth and where he after the conclusion of his wandering went into the earth again, where he dwells to this day.
24 *raiankama* = to produce vibrating sounds while holding the cupped hand in front of the mouth.
25 *arknanaua* = protected, holy place, the place where the *tjurunga*-woods or -stones are stored. Spencer and Gillen call it *ertnatulunga*.
26 *altjamaltjerama* = to become a hidden body, *i.e.*, to assume another form.
27 *inna* = tree, *ngarra* = eternally standing, *patta* = rock, stone, mountain
28 *rella* = man, person; *ngantja* = hidden in the earth, also subterranean. Thus the spring water which is hidden under the sand in the great water courses is called *kwatja ngantja*, *i.e.*, the water hidden in the earth.
29 *ralpara* = dark, underground cave.
30 *knanakala* = has arisen by itself, *i.e.*, conception-place.
31 *patta* = rock, *kalkna* = split, fissure, crack; *patta kalkna* = split rock
32 *manga* = fly; *erkuma* = to capture, to snatch, to catch at; *erkunjerkunja* = catcher; *Mangarkunjerkunja* = the fly-catcher.
33 *itjarama* = to sever, to slit open
34 *altjurilama* = to make a hole, to open
35 Here lived ages ago an influential chieftain who because of his corpulence, which is extremely uncommon amongst the natives, had the name Jabalpa = fat-belly.
36 Here in ancient times a young man (*rukuta*) had ignited a fire which assumed immense dimensions; the sparks flew as far as Ngodna [fire-flame], nowadays called Horseshoe-Bend (so-called because it is situated on a horseshoe-shaped bend of the Finke River).
37 *altanta* = white stone, a form of limestone which is found there.
38 Alice Springs, a telegraph station on the overland telegraph line, situated in the MacDonnell ranges.

39 From *kuja* = boy. Kujunba lies between Alice Springs and Owen Springs situated to the south on the Hugh River; the latter locale is called Nenkakuna because many *nenka* [diamond finches] sojourned there.
40 *albelta* = white, transparent creeksand, since in this place only a few rubber trees stand.
41 *tunga* = perhaps, maybe. Here lived ages ago *tjunba* (*Varanus giganteus* [Gray])-men who did not know whether other *tjunba*-people would come to them or not.
42 *arkularkua* is an owl-like nocturnal bird which at night lets loose a cry reminiscent of the cuckoo, called *kurr-kurr* by the Loritja (Podargus).
43 *Katukankara*, composed of *katu* = *kata* = father, and *inkara* = the not dying, immortal.

The meaning of religion*

Edward Sapir†

A very useful distinction can be made between 'a religion' and 'religion.' The former appears only in a highly developed society in which religious behaviour has been organised by tradition; the latter is universal.

The ordinary conception of a religion includes the notions of a self-conscious 'church,' of religious officers whose functions are clearly defined by custom and who typically engage in no other type of economic activity, and of carefully guarded rituals which are the symbolic expression of the life of the church. Generally, too, such a religion is invested with a certain authority by a canonical tradition which has grown up around a body of sacred texts, supposed to have been revealed by God or to have been faithfully set down by the founder of the religion or by followers of His who have heard the sacred words from His own lips.

If we leave the more sophisticated peoples and study the social habits of primitive and barbaric folk, we shall find that it is very difficult to discover religious institutions that are as highly formalised as those that go under the name of the Roman Catholic Church

---

* First published in *The American Mercury*, 15 (1928): 72-79. This work is in the public domain.

† Edward Sapir, born 1884 in Lauenburg, Prussia (modern day Lębork, Poland), was an American anthropologist and linguist. He is recognised as one of the most important figures in the development of linguistics in the United States, and is known for his work on the indigenous languages of the Americas. He died in 1939.

The meaning of religion

or of Judaism. Yet religion in some sense is everywhere present. It seems to be as universal as speech itself and the use of material tools. It is difficult to apply a single one of the criteria which are ordinarily used to define a religion to the religious behaviour of primitive peoples, yet neither the absence of specific religious officers nor the lack of authoritative religious texts nor any other conventional lack can seriously mislead the student into denying them true religion. Ethnologists are unanimous in ascribing religious behaviour to the very simplest of known societies. So much of a commonplace, indeed, is this assumption of the presence of religion in every known community—barring none, not even those that flaunt the banner of atheism—that one needs to reaffirm and justify the assumption.

How are we to define religion? Can we get behind priests and prayers and gods and rituals and discover a formula that is not too broad to be meaningless nor so specific as to raise futile questions of exclusion or inclusion? I believe it is possible to do this if we ignore for a moment the special forms of behaviour deemed religious and attend to the essential meaning and function of such behaviour. Religion is precisely one of those words that belong to the more intuitive portion of our vocabulary. We can often apply it safely and unexpectedly without the slightest concern for whether the individual or group termed religious is priest-ridden or not, is addicted to prayer or not, or believes or does not believe in a god. Almost unconsciously the term has come to have for most of us a certain connotation of personality. Some individuals are religious and others are not, and all societies have religion in the sense that they provide the naturally religious person with certain ready-made symbols for the exercise of his religious need.

The formula that I would venture to suggest is simply this: Religion is man's never-ceasing attempt to discover a road to spiritual serenity across the perplexities and dangers of daily life. How this serenity is obtained is a matter of infinitely varied detail. Where the need for such serenity is passionately felt, we have religious yearning; where it is absent, religious behaviour is no more than socially sanctioned form or an aesthetic blend of belief and gesture. In practice it is all but impossible to disconnect religious sentiment from formal religious conduct, but it is worth divorcing the two in order that we may insist all the more clearly on the reality of the sentiment.

What constitutes spiritual serenity must be answered afresh for every culture and for every community — in the last analysis, for every individual. Culture defines for every society the world in which it lives, hence we can expect no more of any religion than that it awaken and overcome the feeling of danger, of individual helplessness, that is proper to that particular world. The ultimate problems of an Ojibwe Indian[1] are different as to content from those of the educated devotee of modern science, but with each of them religion means the haunting realisation of ultimate powerlessness in an inscrutable world, and the unquestioning and thoroughly irrational conviction of the possibility of gaining mystic security by somehow identifying oneself with what can never be known. Religion is omnipresent fear and a vast humility paradoxically turned into bedrock security, for once the fear is imaginatively taken to one's heart and the humility confessed for good and all, the triumph of human consciousness is assured. There can be neither fear nor humiliation for deeply religious natures, for they have intuitively experienced both of these emotions in advance of the declared hostility of an overwhelming world, coldly indifferent to human desire.

Religion of such purity as I have defined it is hard to discover. That does not matter; it is the pursuit, conscious or unconscious, of ultimate serenity following total and necessary defeat that constitutes the core of religion. It has often allied itself with art and science, and art at least has gained from the alliance, but in crucial situations religion has always shown itself indifferent to both. Religion seeks neither the objective enlightenment of science nor the strange equilibrium, the sensuous harmony, of æsthetic experience. It aims at nothing more nor less than the impulsive conquest of reality, and it can use science and art as little more than stepping stones toward the attainment of its own serenity. The mind that is intellectualist through and through is necessarily baffled by religion, and in the attempt to explain it makes little more of it than a blind and chaotic science.

Whether or not the spirit of religion is reconcilable with that of art does not concern us. Human nature is infinitely complex and every type of reconciliation of opposites seems possible, but it must be insisted that the nucleus of religious feeling is by no means identical with æsthetic emotion. The serenity of art seems of an utterly different nature from that of religion. Art creates a feeling of wholeness precipitating the flux of things into tangible forms, beautiful and sufficient to themselves; religion gathers up all the threads and meaninglessnesses of life into a wholeness that is not manifest and can only be experienced in the form of a passionate desire. It is not useful and it is perhaps not wise to insist on fundamental antinomies, but if one were pressed to the wall one might perhaps be far from wrong in suspecting that the religious spirit is antithetical to that of art, for religion is essentially ultimate and irreconcilable. Art forgives because it values as an ultimate good the here and now; religion forgives because the here and now are somehow irrelevant to a desire that drives for ultimate solutions.

II

Religion does not presuppose a definite belief in God or in a number of gods or spirits, though in practice such beliefs are generally the rationalised background for religious behaviour.

Belief, as a matter of fact, is not a properly religious concept at all, but a scientific one. The sum total of one's beliefs may be said to constitute one's science. Some of these beliefs can be sustained by an appeal to direct personal experience, others rest for their warrant on the authority of society or on the authority of such individuals as are known or believed to hold in their hands the keys of final demonstration. So far as the normal individual is concerned, a belief in the reality of molecules or atoms is of exactly the same nature as a belief in God or immortality. The true division here is not between science and religious belief, but between personally verifiable and personally unverifiable belief. A philosophy of life is not religion if the phrase connotes merely a cluster of rationalised beliefs. Only when one's philosophy of life is vitalised by emotion does it take on the character of religion.

Some writers have spoken of a specifically religious emotion, but it seems quite unnecessary to appeal to any such hypothetical concept. One may rest content to see in religious emotion nothing more nor less than a cluster of such typical emotional experiences as fear, awe, hope, love, the pleading attitude, and any others that may be experienced, in so far as these psychological experiences occur in a context of ultimate values. Fear as such, no matter how poignant or ecstatic, is not religion. A calm belief in a God who creates and rewards and punishes does not constitute religion if the believer fails to recognise the necessity of the application of this belief to his personal problems. Only when the emotion of fear and the belief in a God are somehow integrated into a value can either the emotion or the belief be said to be of a religious nature. This standpoint allows for no specific religious emotions nor does it recognise any specific forms of belief as necessary for religion. All that is asked is that intensity of feeling join with a philosophy of ultimate things into an unanalysed conviction of the possibility of security in a world of values.

One can distinguish, in theory if not in practice, between individual religious experience and socialised religious behaviour. Some writers on religion put the emphasis on the reality and intensity of the individual experience, others prefer to see in religion a purely social pattern, an institution on which the individual must draw in order to have religious experience at all. The contrast between these two points of view is probably more apparent than real. The suggestions for religious behaviour will always be found to be of social origin; it is the validation of this behaviour in individual or in social terms that may be thought to vary. This is equivalent to saying that some societies tend to seek the most intense expression of religious experience in individual behaviour (including introspection under that term), while others tend toward a collective orthodoxy, reaching an equivalent intensity of life in forms of behaviour in which the individual is subordinated to a collective symbol. Religions that con-

The meaning of religion

form to the first tendency may be called evangelistic, and those of the second type ritualistic.

The contrast invites criticism, as everyone who has handled religious data knows. One may object that it is precisely under the stimulation of collective activity, as in the sun dance of the Plains Indians[2] or in the Roman Catholic mass, that the most intense forms of individual experience are created. Again, one may see in the most lonely and self-centered of religious practices, say the mystic ecstasies of a saint or the private prayer of one lost to society, little more than the religious behaviour of society itself, disconnected, for the moment, from the visible church. A theorist like Durkheim sees the church implicit in every prayer or act of ascetic piety. It is doubtful if the mere observation of religious behaviour quite justifies the distinction that I have made. A finer psychological analysis would probably show that the distinction is none the less valid—that societies differ or tend to differ according to whether they find the last court of appeal in matters religious, in the social act, or in the private emotional experience.

Let one example do for many. The religion of the Plains Indians is different in many of its details from that of the Pueblo Indians of the Southwest.[3] Nevertheless there are many external resemblances between them, such as the use of shrines with fetishistic objects gathered in them, the colour symbolism of cardinal points, and the religious efficacy of communal dancing. It is not these and a host of other resemblances, however, that impress the student of native American religion; it is rather their profound psychological difference. The Plains Indians' religion is full of collective symbols; indeed, a typical ethnological account of the religion of a Plains tribe seems to be little more than a list of social stereotypes—dances and regalia and taboos and conventional religious tokens. The sun dance is an exceedingly elaborate ritual which lasts many days and in which each song and each step in the progress of the ceremonies is a social expression. For all that, the final validation of the sun dance, as of every other form of Plains religion, seems to rest with the individual in his introspective loneliness. The nuclear idea is the 'blessing' or 'manitou' experience, in which the individual puts himself in a relation of extreme intimacy with the world of supernatural power or 'medicine.'

Completely socialised rituals are not the primary fact in the structure of Plains religion; they are rather an extended form of the nuclear individual experience. The recipient of a blessing may and does invite others to participate in the private ritual which has grown up around the vision in which power and security have been vouchsafed to him; he may even transfer his interest in the vision to another individual; in the course of time the original ritual, complicated by many accretions, may become a communal form in which the whole tribe has the most lively and anxious interest, as is the case with the beaver bundle[4] or medicine pipe ceremonies of the Blackfoot Indians.[5] A non-religious individual may see little but show and outward circumstance in all this business of vision and bundle and ritual, but the religious consciousness of the Plains Indians never seems to lose sight of the inherently individual warrant of the vision and of all rituals which may eventually flow from it. It is highly significant that even in the sun dance, which is probably the least individualised kind of religious conduct among these Indians, the highwater mark of religious intensity is felt to reside, not in any collective ecstasy, but in the individual emotions of those who gaze at the centre pole of the sun dance lodge and, still more, of the resolute few who are willing to experience the unspeakably painful ecstasy of self-torture.

The Pueblo religion seems to offer very much of a contrast to the religion of the Plains. The Pueblo religion is ritualised to an incredible degree. Ceremony follows relentlessly on ceremony, clan and religious fraternity go through their stately symbolism of dance and prayer and shrine construction with the regularity of the seasons. All is anxious care for the norm and detail of ritual. But it is not the mere bulk of this ritualism which truly characterises the religion of the Hopi or Zuñi.[6] It is the depersonalised, almost cosmic, quality of the rituals, which have all the air of preordained things of nature which the individual is helpless either to assist or to thwart, and whose mystic intention he can only comprehend by resigning himself to the traditions of his tribe and clan and fraternity. No private intensity of religious experience will help the ritual. Whether the dancer is aroused to a strange ecstasy or remains as cold as an automaton is a matter of perfect indifference to the Pueblo consciousness. All taint of the orgiastic is repudiated by the Pueblo Indian, who is content with the calm constraint and power of things ordained, seeing in himself no discoverer of religious virtue, but only a correct and measured transmitter of things perfect in themselves. One might teach Protestant revivalism to a Blackfoot or a Sioux; a Zuñi would smile uncomprehendingly.

III

Though religion cannot be defined in terms of belief, it is none the less true that the religions of primitive peoples tend to cluster around a number of typical beliefs or classes of belief. It will be quite impossible to give even a superficial account of the many types of religious belief that have been reported for primitive man, and I shall therefore be content with a brief mention of three of them: belief in spirits (animism), belief in gods, and belief in cosmic power (mana).

That primitive peoples are animistic—in other words, that they believe in the existence in the world and in themselves of a vast number of immaterial and potent essences—is a commonplace of anthropology. Tylor[7] attempted to derive all forms of religious behaviour from animistic beliefs, and while we can no longer attach as great an importance to animism as did Tylor and others of the classical anthropologists, it is still correct to say that few primitive religions do not at some point or other connect with the doctrine of spirits. Most peoples believe in a soul which animates the human body; some believe in a variety of souls (as when the principle of life is distinguished from what the psychologists would call consciousness or the psyche); and most peoples also believe in the survival of the soul after death in the form of a ghost.

The experiences of the soul or souls typically account for such phenomena as dreams, illness, and death. Frequently one or another type of soul is identified with such insubstantial things as the breath,

Synkrētic

or the shadow cast by a living being, or, more materially, with such parts of the human body as the heart or diaphragm; sometimes, too, the soul is symbolised by an imaginary being, such as a mannikin, who may leave the body and set out in pursuit of another soul. The mobile soul and the ghost tend to be identified, but this is not necessarily the case.

In all this variety of primitive belief we see little more than the dawn of psychology. The religious attitude enters in only when the soul or ghost is somehow connected with the great world of non-human spirits which animates the whole of nature and which is possessed of a power for good or ill which it is the constant aim of human beings to capture for their own purposes. These 'spirits,' which range all the way from disembodied human souls, through animals, to god-like creatures, are perhaps more often feared than directly worshipped. On the whole, it is perhaps correct to say that spirits touch humanity through the individual rather than through the group and that access is gained to them rather through the private, selfish ritual of magic than through religion. All such generalisations, however, are exceedingly dangerous. Almost any association of beliefs and attitudes is possible.

Tylor believed that the series: soul, ghost, spirit, god, was a necessary genetic chain. 'God' would be no more than the individualised totality of all spirits, localised in earth or air or sea and specialised as to function or kind of power. The single 'god' of a polytheistic pantheon would be the transition stage between the unindividualised spirit and the Supreme Being of the great historical religions. These simple and plausible connections are no longer lightly taken for granted by the anthropologists. There is a great deal of disturbing evidence which seems to show that the idea of a god or of God is not necessarily to be considered as the result of an evolution of the idea of soul or spirit. It would seem that some of the most primitive peoples we know of have arrived at the notion of an all powerful being who stands quite outside the world of spirits and who tends to be identified with such cosmic objects as the sun or the sky.

The Nootka Indians of British Columbia, for instance, believe in the existence of a Supreme Being whom they identify with daylight

The meaning of religion

and who is sharply contrasted both with the horde of mysterious beings ('spirits') from whom they seek power for special ends and with the mythological beings of legend and ritual. Some form of primitive monotheism not infrequently coexists with animism. Polytheism is not necessarily the forerunner of monotheism, but may, for certain culture, be looked upon as a complex, systematised product of several regional ideas of God.

The idea of 'mana,' or diffused, non-individualised power, seems to be exceedingly widespread among primitive peoples. The term has been borrowed from Melanesia, but it is as applicable to the Algonquian, Iroquois, Siouan, and numerous other tribes of aboriginal America as to the Melanesians and Polynesians. The whole world is believed to be pervaded by a mysterious potency that may be concentrated in particular objects or, in many cases, possessed by spirits or animals or gods. Man needs to capture some of this power in order to attain his desires. He is ever on the lookout for blessings from the unknown, which may be vouchsafed to him in unusual or uncanny experiences, in visions, and in dreams. The notion of immaterial power often takes curious forms. Thus the Hupa Indians of Northwestern California believe in the presence of radiations which stream to earth from mysterious realms beyond, inhabited by a supernatural and holy folk who once lived upon earth but vanished with the coming of the Indians. These radiations may give the medicine-woman her power or they may inspire one with the spirit of a ritual.

I can hardly do more than mention some of the typical forms of religious behaviour, as distinguished from belief, which are of universal distribution. Prayer is common, but it is only in the higher reaches of culture that it attains its typically pure and altruistic form. On lower levels it tends to be limited to the voicing of selfish wants, which may even bring harm to those who are not members of one's own household. It is significant that prayers are frequently addressed to specific beings who may grant power or withhold ill rather than to the Supreme Being, even when such a being is believed to exist.

Synkrētic

A second type of religious behaviour is the pursuit of power or 'medicine.' The forms which this pursuit take are exceedingly varied. The individual 'medicine' experience is perhaps illustrated in its greatest purity among the American aborigines, but it is of course plentifully illustrated in other parts of the world. Among some tribes the receipt of power, which generally takes place in the form of a dream or vision, establishes a very personal relation between the giver of the blessing and the suppliant.

This relation is frequently known as individual totemism. The term totemism, indeed, is derived from the Ojibwe Indians, among whom there is a tendency for the individual to be 'blessed' by the same supernatural beings as have already blessed his paternal ancestors. Such an example as this shows how the purely individual relation may gradually become socialised into the institution typically known as totemism, which may be defined as a specific relation, manifested in a great variety of ways, which exists between a clan or other social group and a supernatural being, generally, but by no means exclusively, identified with an animal. In spite of the somewhat shadowy borderland which connects individual totemism with group totemism, it is inadvisable to think of the one institution as necessarily derived from the other, though the possibility of such a development need not be denied outright.

Closely connected with the pursuit of power is the handling of magical objects or assemblages of such objects which contained or symbolise the power that has been bestowed. Among some of the North American Indian tribes, as we have seen, the 'medicine bundle,' with its associated ritual and taboos, owes its potency entirely to the supernatural experience which lies back of it. Classical fetishism, however, as we find it in West Africa, seems not to be necessarily based on an individual vision. A fetish is an object which possesses power in its own right and which may be used to affect desired ends by appropriate handling, prayer, or other means. In many cases a supernatural being is believed to be actually resident in the fetish, though this conception, which most nearly corresponds to the popular notion of 'idol,' is probably not as common as might be expected. The main religious significance of medicine

The meaning of religion

bundles, fetishes and other tokens of the supernatural is the reassuring power exerted on the primitive mind by a concrete symbol which is felt to be closely connected with the mysterious unknown and its limitless power. It is of course the persistence of the suggestibility of visual symbols which makes even the highest forms of religion tend to cluster about such objects as temples, churches, shrines, crucifixes, and the like.

The fourth and perhaps the most important of the forms of religious behaviour is the carrying out of rituals. Rituals are typically symbolic actions which belong to the whole community, but among primitive peoples there is a tendency for many of them to be looked upon as the special function of a limited group within the whole tribe. Sometimes this group is a clan or gens or other division not based on religious concepts; at other times the group is a religious fraternity, a brotherhood of priests, which exists for the sole purpose of seeing to the correct performance of rituals which are believed to be of the utmost consequence for the safety of the tribe as a whole. It is difficult to generalise about primitive ritual, so varied are the forms which it assumes. Nearly everywhere the communal ritual whips the whole tribe into a state of great emotional tension, which is interpreted by the folk as a visitation from the supernatural world. The most powerful means known to bring about this feeling is the dance, which is nearly always accompanied by singing.

Some ethnologists have seen in primitive ritual little more than the counterpart of our own dramatic and pantomimic performances. Historically there is undoubtedly much truth in this but it would be very misleading to make of a psychology of primitive ritual a mere chapter in the psychology of æsthetic experience. The exaltation of the Sioux sun dancer or of a Northwest Coast Indian who impersonates the Cannibal Spirit is a very different thing from the excitement of the performing artist. It seems very much more akin to the intense reverie of the mystic or ascetic. Externally, the ritual may be described as a sacred drama; subjectively, it may bring the participant to a realisation of mystery and power for which the fetish or other religious object is but an external token. The psychological interpretation of ritual naturally differs with the temperament of the individual.

IV

The sharp distinction between religious and other modes of conduct to which we are accustomed in modern life is by no means possible on more primitive levels. Religion is neither ethics nor science nor art, but it tends to be inextricably bound up with all three. It also manifests itself in the social organisation of the tribe, in ideas of higher or lower status, in the very form and technique of government itself. It is sometimes said that it is impossible to disentangle religious behaviour among primitive peoples from the setting in which it is found. For many primitives, however, it seems almost more correct to say that religion is the one structural reality in the whole of their culture and that what we call art and ethics and science and social organisation are hardly more than the application of the religious point of view to the functions of daily life.

In concluding, attention may be called to the wide distribution of certain sentiments or feelings which are of a peculiarly religious nature and which tend to persist even among the most sophisticated individuals, long after they have ceased to believe in the rationalised justification for these sentiments and feelings. They are by no means to be identified with simple emotions, though they obviously feed on the soil of all emotions. A religious sentiment is typically unconscious, intense, and bound up with a compulsive sense of values. It is possible that modern psychology may analyse them all away as socialised compulsion neuroses, but it is exceedingly doubtful if a healthy social life or a significant individual life is possible without these very sentiments. The first and most important of them is a 'feeling of community with a necessary universe of values.' In psychological terms, this feeling seems to be a blend of complete humility and a no less complete security. It is only when the fundamental serenity is as intense as fear and as necessary as any of the simpler sentiments that its possessor can be properly termed a mystic.

The meaning of religion

A second sentiment, which often grows out of the first, is a feeling for sacredness or holiness or divinity. That certain experiences or ideas or objects or personalities must be set apart as symbols of ultimate value is an idea which is repellent to the critical modern mind. It is none the less a necessary sentiment to many, perhaps to most, human beings. The consciously justified infraction of sentiments of holiness, which cannot be recognised by the thinking mind, leads frequently to an inexplicable personal unhappiness.

The taboos of primitive peoples strike us as very bizarre and it is a commonplace of psychoanalysis that many of them have a strange kinship with the apparently self-imposed taboos of neurotics. It is doubtful if many psychologists or students of culture realise the psychological significance of taboo, which seems nothing more nor less than an unconscious striving for the strength that comes from any form of sacrifice or deferment of immediate fulfillments. Certainly all religions have insisted on the importance of both taboo, in its narrower sense of specific interdiction, and sacrifice. It may be that the feeling of the necessity of sacrifice is no more than a translation into action of the sentiment of the holy.

Perhaps the most difficult of the religious sentiments to understand is that of sin, which is almost amusingly abhorrent to the modern mind. Every constellation of sentiments holds within itself its own opposites. The more intense a sentiment, the more certain is the potential presence of a feeling which results from the flouting or thwarting of it. The price for the reality and intensity of the positive sentiments that I have mentioned, any or all of which must of necessity be frequently violated in the course of daily life, is the sentiment of sin, which is a necessary shadow cast by all sincerely religious feeling.

It is, of course, no accident that religion in its most authentic moments has always been prepared to cancel a factual shortcoming in conduct if only it could assure itself that this shortcoming was accompanied by a lively sense of sin. Good works are not the equivalent of the sentiment of ultimate value which religion insists upon. The shadow cast by this sentiment, which is a sense of sin, may be intuitively felt as of more reassuring value than a benevol-

Synkrētic

ence which proceeds from mere social habit or from personal indifference. Religion has always been the enemy of self-satisfaction.

Notes

1 *Ojibwe (also Ojibwa, Ojibway, Chippewa)*: an indigenous American people of the Great Lakes region and northern plains of the United States and Canada.
2 *Sun dance of the Plains Indians*: a ceremony central to the religious identity of the Indigenous peoples of the Great Plains. The name 'sun dance' derives from the Sioux name for the cermony, *Wi wanyang wacipi* or 'sun gazing dance'. See 'Sun Dance' in the Encyclopedia of the Great Plains: <http://plainshumanities.unl.edu/encyclopedia/doc/egp.rel.046.>
3 *Pueblo Indians of the South West*: known also as Puebloans, are an indigenous American cultural group consisting of multiple tribes which have agricultural, material, and religious practices in common.
4 *Beaver bundle*: a wrapped collection of sacred items (sacred bundle, medicine bundle) of the Blackfoot Indians.
5 *Blackfoot Indians*: an indigenous American people whose traditional lands span parts of southern Alberta and Saskatchewan in Canada, and northern Monatana in the United States. See the website of the Blackfeet Nation: <https://blackfeetnation.com/>
6 *Hopi or Zuñi*: Pueblo Indian groups of New Mexico and northeastern Arizona, respectively. Modern spelling: Zuni.
7 *Tylor*: Sir Edward Burnett Tylor (1832-1917), English anthropologist who reintroduced the term 'animism' into common use. He regarded animism as the first phase in the development of religions, as set out in his work *Primitive Culture* (1871), of which an extract appears on the following pages.

45

Animism*

Edward Burnett Tylor†

Are there, or have there been, tribes of men so low in culture as to have no religious conceptions whatever? This is practically the question of the universality of religion, which for so many centuries has been affirmed and denied, with a confidence in striking contrast to the imperfect evidence on which both affirmation and denial have been based. Ethnographers, if looking to a theory of development to explain civilisation, and regarding its successive stages as arising one from another, would receive with peculiar interest accounts of tribes devoid of all religion. Here, they would naturally say, are men who have no religion because their forefathers had none, men who represent a pre-religious condition of the human race, out of which in the course of time religious conditions have arisen. It does not, however, seem advisable to start from this ground in an investigation of religious development. Though the theoretical niche is ready and convenient, the actual statue to fill it is not forthcoming. The case is in some degree similar to that of the tribes asserted to exist

---

* This is an extract from chapter XI ('Animism'), volume 1 of Edward Burnett Tylor's *Primitive Culture: Researches into the Development of Mythology, Philosophy, Religion, Language, Art and Custom*, 6e (London: John Murray, 1920). This work is in the public domain and available on archive.org. It is reproduced here with minor edits to modernise or standardise the orthography. No edits have been made where these could be seen to alter the historical or intellectual character of the text. The endnotes are the author's, except where indicated.

† Edward Burnett Tylor (1832-1917) was an English anthropologist whose ideas were typical of the theories of cultural evolutionism which dominated 19th century social thought.

without language or without the use of fire; nothing in the nature of things seems to forbid the possibility of such existence, but as a matter of fact the tribes are not found. Thus the assertion that rude non-religious tribes have been known in actual existence, though in theory possible, and perhaps in fact true, does not at present rest on that sufficient proof which, for an exceptional state of things, we are entitled to demand.

It is not unusual for the very writer who declares in general terms the absence of religious phenomena among some savage people, himself to give evidence that shows his expressions to be misleading. Thus Dr Lang not only declares that the aborigines of Australia have no idea of a supreme divinity, creator, and judge, no object of worship, no idol, temple, or sacrifice, but that 'in short, they have nothing whatever of the character of religion, or of religious observance, to distinguish them from the beasts that perish.' More than one writer has since made use of this telling statement, but without referring to certain details which occur in the very same book. From these it appears that a disease like smallpox, which sometimes attacks the natives, is ascribed by them 'to the influence of Budyah, an evil spirit who delights in mischief'; that when the natives rob a wild bees' hive, they generally leave a little of the honey for Buddai; that at certain biennial gatherings of the Queensland tribes, young girls are slain in sacrifice to propitiate some evil divinity; and that, lastly, according to the evidence of the Rev. W. Ridley, 'whenever he has conversed with the aborigines, he found them to have definite traditions concerning supernatural beings — Baiame, whose voice they hear in thunder, and who made all things, Turramullum the chief of demons, who is the author of disease, mischief, and wisdom, and appears in the form of a serpent at their great assemblies, etc.'[1] By the concurring testimony of a crowd of observers, it is known that the natives of Australia were at their discovery, and have since remained, a race with minds saturated with the most vivid belief in souls, demons, and deities. In Africa, Mr Moffat's declaration as to the Bechuanas is scarcely less surprising — that 'man's immortality was never heard of among that people,' he having remarked in the sentence next before, that the word for the shades or manes of the dead 'liriti.'[2] In South America, again, Don Felix de Azara comments on the positive falsity of the ecclesiastics' assertion that the native tribes have a religion. He simply declares that they have none; nevertheless in the course of his work he mentions such facts as that the Payaguas bury arms and clothing with their dead and have some notions of a future life, and that the Guanas believe in a Being who rewards good and punishes evil. In fact, this author's reckless denial of religion and law to the lower races of this region justifies D'Orbigny's sharp criticism, that, 'this is indeed what he says of all the nations he describes, while actually proving the contrary of his thesis by the very facts he alleges in its support.'[3]

Such cases show how deceptive are judgments to which breadth and generality are given by the use of wide words in narrow senses. Lang, Moffat, and Azara are authors to whom ethnography owes much valuable knowledge of the tribes they visited, but they seem hardly to have recognised anything short of the organised and established theology of the higher races as being religion at all. They attribute irreligion to tribes whose doctrines are unlike theirs, in much the same manner as theologians have so often attributed atheism to those whose deities differed from their own, from thee time when the ancient invading Aryans described the aboriginal tribes of India as *adeva*, *i.e.*, 'godless,' and the Greeks fixed the corresponding term άθεοι on the early Christians as unbelievers in the classic gods, to the comparatively modern ages when disbelievers in witchcraft and apostolical succession were denounced as atheists; and down to our own day, when controversialists are apt to infer, as in past centuries, that naturalists who support a theory of development of species therefore necessarily hold atheistic opinions.[4] These are in fact but examples of a general perversion of judgment in theological matters, among the results of which is a popular misconception of the religions of the lower races, simply amazing to students who have reached a higher point of view. Some missionaries, no doubt, thoroughly understand the minds of the savages they have to deal with, and indeed it is from men like Cranz, Dobrizhoffer, Charlevoix, Ellis, Hardy, Callaway, J. L. Wilson, T. Williams, that we have obtained our best knowledge of the lower phases of religious belief. But for the most part the 'religious world' is so occupied in hating and despising the beliefs of the heathen whose vast regions of the globe are painted black on the missionary maps, that they have little time or capacity left to understand them. It cannot be so with those who fairly seek to comprehend the nature and meaning of the lower phases of religion. These, while fully alive to the absurdities believed and the horrors perpetrated in its name, will yet regard with kindly interest all record of men's earnest seeking after truth with such light as they could find. Such students will look for meaning, however crude and childish, at the root of doctrines often most dark to the believers who accept them most zealously; they will search for the reasonable thought which once gave life to observances now become in seeming or reality the most abject and superstitious folly. The reward of these enquirers will be a more rational comprehension of the faiths in whose midst they dwell, for no more can he who understands but one religion understand even that religion, than the man who knows but one language can understand that language. No religion of mankind lies in utter isolation from the rest, and the thoughts and principles of modern Christianity are attached to intellectual clues which run back through far pre-Christian ages to the very origin of human civilisation, perhaps even of human existence.

While observers who have had fair opportunities of studying the religion of savages have thus sometimes done scant justice to the facts before their eyes, the hasty denials of others who have judged without even facts can carry no great weight. A 16th century traveller gave an account of the natives of Florida which is typical of such: 'Touching the religion of this people, which wee have found, for want of their language wee could not understand neither by signs nor gesture that they had any religion or lawe at all. ... We suppose that they have no religion at all, and that they live at their own libertie.'[5] Better knowledge of these Floridans nevertheless showed that they had a religion, and better knowledge has reversed many another hasty assertion to the same effect; as when writers used to declare that the natives of Madagascar had no idea of a future state, and no word for soul or spirit;[6] or when Dampier enquired after the religion of the natives of Timor, and was told that they had none;[7] or when Sir Thomas Roe landed in Saldanha Bay on his way to the court of the Great Mogul, and remarked of the Hottentots[8] that 'they have left off their custom of stealing, but know no God or religion.'[9] Among the numerous accounts collected by Lord Avebury as evidence bearing on the absence or low development of religion among low races,[10] some may be selected as lying open to criticism from this point of view. Thus the statement that the Samoan Islanders had no religion cannot stand, in face of the elaborate description by the Rev. G. Turner of the Samoan religion itself; and the assertion that the Tupinambas of Brazil had no religion is one not to be received on merely negative evidence, for the religious doctrines and practices of the Tupi race have been recorded by Lery, De Laet, and other writers. Even with much time and care and knowledge of language, it is not always easy to elicit from savages the details of their theology. They try to hide from the prying and contemptuous foreigner their worship of gods who seem to shrink, like their worshippers, before the white man and his mightier Deity. Mr Sproat's experience in Vancouver's Island is an apt example of this state of things. He says: 'I was two years among the Ahts,[11] with my mind constantly directed towards the subject of their religious beliefs, before I could discover that they possessed any ideas as to an overruling power or a future state of existence. The traders on the coast, and other persons well acquainted with the people, told me that they had no such ideas, and this opinion was confirmed by conversation with many of the less intelligent savages; but at last I succeeded in getting a satisfactory clue.'[12] It then appeared that the Ahts had all the time been hiding a whole characteristic system of religious doctrines as to souls and their migrations, the spirits who do good and ill to men, and the great gods above all. Thus, even where no positive proof of religious ideas among any particular tribe has reached us, we should distrust its denial by observers whose acquaintance with the tribe in question has not been intimate as well as kindly. It is said of the Andaman Islanders that they have not the rudest elements of a religious faith; yet it appears that the natives did not even display to the foreigners the rude music which they actually possessed, so that they could scarcely have been expected to be communicative as to their theology, if they had any.[13] In our time the most striking negation of the religion of savage tribes is that published by Sir Samuel Baker, in a paper read in 1866 before the Ethnological Society of London, as follows: 'The most northern tribes of the White Nile are the Dinkas, Shillooks, Nuehr, Kytch, Bohr, Aliab, and Shir. A general description will suffice for the whole, excepting the Kytch. Without any exception, they are without a belief in a Supreme Being, neither have they any form of worship or idolatry; nor is the darkness of their minds enlightened by even a ray of superstition.' Had this distinguished explorer spoken only of the Latukas, or of other tribes hardly known to ethnographers except through his own intercourse with them, his denial of any religious consciousness to them would have been at least entitled to stand as the best procurable account, until more intimate communication should prove or disprove it. But in speaking thus of comparatively well known tribes such as the Dinkas, Shilluks and Nuehr, Sir S. Baker ignores the existence of published evidence, such as describes the sacrifices of the Dinkas, their belief in good and evil spirits (*adjok* and *djyok*), their good deity and heaven-dwelling creator, *Dendid*, as likewise *Néar* the Deity of the Nuehr, and the Shilluk's creator, who is described as visiting, like other spirits, a sacred wood or tree. Kaufmann, Brun-Rollet, Lejean, and other observers, had thus placed on record details of the religion of these White Nile tribes, years before Sir S. Baker's rash denial that they had any religion at all.[14]

The first requisite in a systematic study of the religions of the lower races, is to lay down a rudimentary definition of religion. By requiring in this definition the belief in a supreme deity or of judgment after death, the adoration of idols or the practice of sacrifice, or other partially diffused doctrines or rites, no doubt many tribes may be excluded from the category of religious. But such narrow definition has the fault of identifying religion rather with particular developments than with the deeper motive which underlies them. It seems best to fall back at once on this essential source, and simply

Animism

to claim, as a minimum definition of Religion, the belief in Spiritual Beings. If this standard be applied to the descriptions of low races as to religion, the following results will appear. It cannot be positively asserted that every existing tribe recognises the belief in spiritual beings, for the native condition of a considerable number is obscure in this respect, and from the rapid change or extinction they are undergoing, may ever remain so. It would be yet more unwarranted to set down every tribe mentioned in history, or known to us by the discovery of antiquarian relics, as necessarily having passed the defined minimum of religion. Greater still would be the unwisdom of declaring such a rudimentary belief natural or instinctive in all human tribes of all times; for no evidence justifies the opinion that man, known to be capable of so vast an intellectual development, cannot have emerged from a non-religious condition, previous to that religious condition in which he happens at present to come with sufficient clearness within our range of knowledge. It is desirable, however, to take our basis of enquiry in observation rather than from speculation. Here, so far as I can judge from the immense mass of accessible evidence, we have to admit that the belief in spiritual beings appears among all low races with whom we have attained to thoroughly intimate acquaintance; whereas the assertion of absence of such belief, must apply either to ancient tribes, or to more or less imperfectly described modern ones. The exact bearing of this state of things on the problem of the origin of religion may be thus briefly stated. Were it distinctly proved that non-religious savages exist or have existed, these might be at least plausibly claimed as representatives of the condition of Man before he arrived at the religious state of culture. It is not desirable, however, that this argument should be put forward, for the asserted existence of the non-religious tribes in question rests, as we have seen, on evidence often mistaken and never conclusive. The argument for the natural evolution of religious ideas among mankind is not invalidated by the rejection of an ally too weak at present to give effectual help. Non-religious tribes may not exist in our day, but the fact bears no more decisively on the development of religion, than the impossibility of finding a modern English village without scis-

Synkrētic

sors or books or lucifer matches bears on the fact that there was a time when no such things existed in the land.

I propose here, under the name of Animism, to investigate the deep-lying doctrine of Spiritual Beings, which embodies the very essence of Spiritualistic as opposed to Materialistic philosophy. Animism is not a new technical term, though now seldom used.[15] From its special relation to the doctrine of the soul, it will be seen to have a peculiar appropriateness to the view here taken of the mode in which theological ideas have been developed among mankind. The word Spiritualism, though it may be, and sometimes is, used in a general sense, has this obvious defect to us, that it has become the designation of a particular modern sect, who indeed hold extreme spiritualistic views, but cannot be taken as typical representatives of these views in the world at large. The sense of Spiritualism in its wider acceptation, the general belief in spiritual beings, is here given to Animism.

Animism characterises tribes very low in the scale of humanity, and thence ascends, deeply modified in its transmission, but from first to last preserving an unbroken continuity, into the midst of high modern culture. Doctrines adverse to it, so largely held by individuals or schools, are usually due not to early lowness of civilisation, but to later changes in the intellectual course, to divergence from, or rejection of, ancestral faiths; and such newer developments do not affect the present enquiry as to the fundamental religious condition of mankind. Animism is, in fact, the groundwork of the Philosophy of Religion, from that of savages up to that of civilised men. And although it may at first sight seem to afford but a bare and meagre definition of a minimum of religion, it will be found practically sufficient; for where the root is, the branches will generally be produced. It is habitually found that the theory of Animism divides into two great dogmas, forming parts of one consistent doctrine; first, concerning souls of individual creatures, capable of continued existence after the death or destruction of the body; second, concerning other spirits, upward to the rank of powerful deities. Spiritual beings are held to affect or control the events of the material world, and man's life here and hereafter; and it being considered that they hold intercourse with men, and receive pleasure or displeasure from human actions, the belief in their existence leads naturally, and it might almost be said inevitably, sooner or later to active reverence and propitiation. Thus Animism in its full development includes the belief in souls and in a future state, in controlling deities and subordinate spirits, these doctrines practically resulting in some kind of active worship. One great element of religion, that moral element which among the higher nations forms its most vital part, is indeed little represented in the religion of the lower races. It is not that these races have no moral sense or no moral standard, for both are strongly marked among them, if not in formal precept, at least in that traditional consensus of society which we call public opinion, according to which certain actions are held to be good or bad, right or wrong. It is that the conjunction of ethics and Animistic philosophy, so intimate and powerful in the higher culture, seems scarcely yet to have begun in the lower. I propose here hardly to touch upon the purely moral aspects of religion, but rather to study the animism of the world so far as it constitutes, as unquestionably it does constitute, an ancient and worldwide philosophy, of which belief is the theory and worship is the practice. Endeavouring to shape the materials for an enquiry hitherto strangely undervalued and neglected, it will now be my task to bring as clearly as may be into view the fundamental animism of the lower races, and in some slight and broken outline to trace its course into higher regions of civilisation. Here let me state once for all two principal conditions under which the present research is carried on. First, as to the religious doctrines and practices examined, these are treated as belonging to theological systems devised by human reason, without supernatural aid or revelation; in other words, as being developments of Natural Religion. Second, as to the connection between similar ideas and rites in the religions of the savage and the civilised world. While dwelling at some length on doctrines and ceremonies of the lower races, and sometimes particularising for special reasons the related doctrines and ceremonies of the higher nations, it has not seemed my proper task to work out in detail the problems thus suggested among the philosophies and creeds of Christendom. Such applications, extending farthest from the direct scope of a work on primitive culture, are briefly stated in general terms, or touched in slight allusion, or taken for granted without remark. Educated readers possess the information required to work out their general bearing on theology, while more technical discussion is left to philosophers and theologians specially occupied with such arguments.

The first branch of the subject to be considered is the doctrine of human and other Souls, an examination of which will occupy the rest of the present chapter. What the doctrine of the soul is among the lower races, may be explained in stating the animistic theory of its development. It seems as though thinking men, as yet at a low level of culture, were deeply impressed by two groups of biological problems. In the first place, what is it that makes the difference between a living body and a dead one; what causes waking, sleep, trance, disease, death? In the second place, what are those human shapes which appear in dreams and visions? Looking at these two groups of phenomena, the ancient savage philosophers probably made their first step by the obvious inference that every man has two things belonging to him, namely, a life and a phantom. These two are evidently in close connection with the body, the life as enabling it to feel and think and act, the phantom as being its image or second self; both, also, are perceived to be things separable from the body, the life as able to go away and leave it insensible or dead, the phantom as appearing to people at a distance from it. The second step would seem also easy for savages to make, seeing how extremely difficult civilised men have found it to unmake. It is merely to combine the life and the phantom. As both belong to the body, why should they not also belong to one another, and be manifestations of one and the same soul? Let them then be considered as united, and the result is that well-known conception which may be described as an apparitional-soul, a ghost-soul. This, at any rate, corresponds with the actual conception of the personal soul or spirit among the lower races, which may be defined as follows: It is a thin unsubstantial human image, in its nature a sort of vapour, film, or shadow; the cause of life and thought in the individual it animates; independently possessing the personal consciousness and volition of its corporeal owner, past or present; capable of leaving the body far behind, to flash swiftly from place to place; mostly impalpable and invisible, yet also manifesting physical power, and especially appearing to men waking or asleep as a phantasm separate from the body of which it bears the likeness; continuing to exist and appear to men after the death of that body; able to enter into, possess, and act in the bodies of other men, of animals, and even of things. Though this definition is by no means of universal application, it has sufficient generality to be taken as a standard, modified by more or less divergence among any particular people. Far from these worldwide opinions being arbitrary or conventional products, it is seldom even justifiable to consider their uniformity among distant races as proving communication of any sort. They are doctrines answering in the most forcible way to the plain evidence of men's senses, as interpreted by a fairly consistent and rational primitive philosophy. So well, indeed, does primitive animism account for the facts of nature, that it has held its place into the higher levels of education. Though classic and mediæval philosophy modified it much, and modern philosophy has handled it yet more unsparingly, it has so far retained the traces of its original character, that heirlooms of primitive ages may be claimed in the existing psychology of the civilised world. Out of the vast mass of evidence, collected among the most various and distant races of mankind, typical details may now be selected to display the earlier theory of the soul, the relation of the parts of this theory, and the manner in which these parts have been abandoned, modified, or kept up, along the course of culture.

To understand the popular conceptions of the human soul or spirit, it is instructive to notice the words which have been found suitable to express it. The ghost or phantasm seen by the dreamer or the visionary is an unsubstantial form, like a shadow or reflection, and thus the familiar term of the *shade* comes in to express the soul. Thus the Tasmanian word for the shadow is also that for the spirit;[16] the Algonquins describe a man's soul as *otahchuk*, 'his shadow;'[17] the Quiché language uses *natub* for 'shadow, soul;'[18] the

Arawak *ueja* means 'shadow, soul, image;'[19] the Abipones made the one word *loákal* serve for 'shadow, soul, echo, image.'[20] The Zulus not only use the word *tunzi* for 'shadow, spirit, ghost,' but they consider that at death the shadow of a man will in some way depart from the corpse, to become an ancestral spirit.[21] The Basutos not only call the spirit remaining after death the *seriti* or 'shadow,' but they think that if a man walks on the river bank, a crocodile may seize his shadow in the water and draw him in;[22] while in Old Calabar there is found the same identification of the spirit with the *ukpon* or 'shadow,' for a man to lose which is fatal.[23] There are thus found among the lower races not only the types of those familiar classic terms, the *skia* and *umbra*, but also what seems the fundamental thought of the stories of shadowless men still current in the folklore of Europe, and familiar to modern readers in Chamisso's tale of Peter Schlemihl. Thus the dead in Purgatory knew that Dante was alive when they saw that, unlike theirs, his figure cast a shadow on the ground.[24] Other attributes are taken into notion of soul or spirit, with especial regard to its being cause of life. Thus the Caribs, connecting the pulses with spiritual beings, and especially considering that in the heart dwells man's chief soul, destined to a future heavenly life, could reasonably use the one word *iouanni* for 'soul, life, heart.'[25] The Tongans supposed the soul to exist throughout the whole extension of the body, but particularly in the heart. On one occasion, the natives were declaring to a European that a man buried months ago was nevertheless still alive. 'And one, endeavouring to make me understand what he meant, took hold of my hand, and squeezing it, said, "This will die, but the life that is within you will never die;" with his other hand pointing to my heart.'[26] So the Basutos say of a dead man that his heart is gone out, and of one recovering from sickness that his heart is coming back.[27] This corresponds to the familiar Old World view of the heart as the prime mover in life, thought, and passion. The connection of soul and blood, familiar to the Karens and Papuas, appears prominently in Jewish and Arabic philosophy.[28] To educated moderns the idea of the Macusi Indians of Guiana may seem quaint, that although the body will decay, 'the man in our eyes' will not die, but wander

Animism

about.²⁹ Yet the association of personal animation with the pupil of the eye is familiar to European folklore, which not unreasonably discerned a sign of bewitchment or approaching death in the disappearance of the image, pupil, or baby, from the dim eyeballs of the sick man.³⁰

The act of breathing, so characteristic of the higher animals during life, and coinciding so closely with life in its departure, has been repeatedly and naturally identified with the life or soul itself. Laura Bridgman showed in her instructive way the analogy between the effects of restricted sense and restricted civilisation, when one day she made the gesture of taking something away from her mouth: 'I dreamed,' she explained in words, 'that God took away my breath to heaven.'³¹ It is thus that West Australians used one word *waug* for 'breath, spirit, soul;'³² that in the Netela language of California, *piuts* means 'life, breath, soul;'³³ that certain Greenlanders reckoned two souls to man, namely his shadow and his breath;³⁴ that the Malays say the soul of the dying man escapes through his nostrils, and in Java use the same word *ñawa* for 'breath, life, soul.'³⁵ How the notions of life, heart, breath, and phantom unite in the one conception of a soul or spirit, and at the same time how loose and vague such ideas are among barbaric races, is well brought into view in the answers to a religious inquest held in 1528 among the natives of Nicaragua. 'When they die, there comes out of their mouth something that resembles a person, and is called *julio* [Aztec *yuli* = to live]. This being goes to the place where the man and woman are. It is like a person, but does not die, and the body remains here.' *Question*. 'Do those who go up on high keep the same body, the same face, and the same limbs, as here below?' *Answer*. 'No; there is only the heart.' *Question*. 'But since they tear out their hearts [*i.e.*, when a captive was sacrificed], what happens then?' *Answer*. 'It is not precisely the heart, but that in them which makes them live, and that quits the body when they die.' Or, as stated in another interrogitory, 'It is not their heart that goes up above, but what makes them live, that is to say, the breath that issues from their mouth and is called *julio*.'³⁶ The conception of the soul as breath may be followed up through Semitic and Aryan etymology, and thus into the main streams of the philosophy of the world. Hebrew shows *nephesh*, 'breath,' passing into all the meanings of 'life, soul, mind, animal,' while *ruach* and *neshamah* make the like transition from 'breath' to 'spirit'; and to these the Arabic *nefs* and *ruh* correspond. The same is the history of Sanskrit *âtman* and *prâna*, of Greek *psychń* and *pneuma*, of Latin *animus, anima, spiritus*. So Slavonic *duch* has developed the meaning of 'breath' into that of soul or spirit; and the dialects of the Gypsies have this word *dūk* with the meanings of 'breath, spirit, ghost,' whether these pariahs brought the word from India as part of their inheritance of Aryan speech, or whether they adopted it in their migration across Slavonic lands.[37] German *Geist* and English *ghost*, too, may possibly have the same original sense of breath. And if any should think such expressions due to mere metaphor, they may judge the strength of the implied connection between breath and spirit by cases of most unequivocal significance. Among the Seminoles of Florida, when a woman died in childbirth, the infant was held over her face to receive her parting spirit, and thus acquire strength and knowledge for its future use. These Indians could have well understood why at the death-bed of an ancient Roman, the nearest kinsman leant over to inhale the last breath of the departing (*et excipies hanc animam ore pio*). Their state of mind is kept up to this day among Tyrolese peasants, who can still fancy a good man's soul to issue from his mouth at death like a little white cloud.[38]

It will be shown that men, in their composite and confused notions of the soul, have brought into connection a list of manifestations of life and thought even more multifarious than this. But also, seeking to avoid such perplexity of combination, they have sometimes endeavoured to define and classify more closely, especially by the theory that man has a combination of several kinds of spirit, soul, or image, to which different functions belong. Already in the barbaric world such classification has been invented or adopted. Thus the Fijians distinguished between a man's 'dark spirit' or shadow, which goes to Hades, and his 'light spirit' or reflection in water or a mirror, which stays near where he dies.[39] The Malagasy say that the *saina* or mind vanishes at death, the *aina* or life becomes

Animism

mere air, but the *matoatoa* or ghost hovers round the tomb.[40] In North America, the duality of the soul is a strongly marked Algonquin belief; one soul goes out and sees dreams while the other remains behind; at death one of the two abides with the body, and for this the survivors leave offerings of food, while the other departs to the land of the dead. A division into three souls is also known, and the Dakotas say that man has four souls, one remaining with the corpse, one staying in the village, one going in the air, and one to the land of spirits.[41] The Karens distinguish between the 'là' or 'kelah,' the personal life-phantom, and the 'thah,' the responsible moral soul.[42] More or less under Hindu influence, the Khonds have a fourfold division, as follows: the first soul is that capable of beatification or restoration to Boora the Good Deity; the second is attached to a Khond tribe on earth and is reborn generation after generation, so that at the birth of each child the priest asks who has returned; the third goes out to hold spiritual intercourse, leaving the body in a languid state, and it is this soul which can pass for a time into a tiger, and transmigrates for punishment after death; the fourth dies on the dissolution of the body.[43] Such classifications resemble those of higher nations, as for instance the threefold division of shade, manes, and spirit:

> Bis duo sunt homini, manes, caro, spiritus, umbra:
> Quatuor ista loci bis duo suscipiunt.
> Terra tegit carnem, tumulum circumvolat umbra,
> Orcus habet manes, spiritus astra petit.
>
> [Four things are man's – flesh, spirit, ghost, and shade;
> And four their final homes: – hell claims the ghost;
> The spirit, heaven; in earth the flesh is laid;
> And, hov'ring o'er it, seeks the shade its post.][44]

Not attempting to follow up the details of such psychical division into the elaborate systems of literary nations, I shall not discuss the distinction which the ancient Egyptians seem to have made in the Ritual of the Dead between the man's *ba, akh, ka, khaba*, translated by Dr Birch as his 'soul,' 'mind,' 'image,' 'shade,' or the Rabbinical division into what may be roughly described as the bod-

Synkrētic

ily, spiritual, and celestial souls, or the distinction between the emanative and genetic souls in Hindu philosophy, or the distribution of life, apparition, ancestral spirit, among the three souls the Chinese, or the demarcations of the *nous, psychē,* and *pneuma,* or of the *anima* and *animus,* or the famous classic and mediæval theories of the vegetal, sensitive, and rational souls. Suffice it to point out here that such speculation dates back to the barbaric condition of our race, in a state fairly comparing as to scientific value with much that gained esteem within the precincts of higher culture. It would be a difficult task to treat such classification on a consistent logical basis. Terms corresponding with those of life, mind, soul, spirit, ghost, and so forth, are not thought as describing really separate entities, so much as the several forms and functions of one individual being. Thus the confusion which here prevails in our own thought and language, in a manner typical of the thought and language of mankind in general, is in fact due not merely to vagueness of terms, but to an ancient theory of substantial unity which underlies them. Such ambiguity of language, however, will be found to interfere little with the present enquiry, for the details given of the nature and action of spirits, souls, phantoms, will themselves define the exact sense such words are to be taken in.

The early animistic theory of vitality, regarding the functions of life as caused by the soul, offers to the savage mind an explanation of several bodily and mental conditions, as being effects of a departure of the soul or some of its constituent spirits. This theory holds a wide and strong position in savage biology. The South Australians express it when they say of one insensible or unconscious, that he is 'wilyamarraba,' *i.e.*, 'without soul.'[45] Among the Algonquin Indians of North America, we hear of sickness being accounted for by the patient's 'shadow' being unsettled or detached from his body, and of the convalescent being reproached for exposing himself before his shadow was safely settled down in him; where we should say that a man was ill and recovered, they would consider that he died, but came again. Another account from among the same race explains the condition of men lying in lethargy or trance; their souls have travelled to the banks of the River of Death, but have been driven back and return to reanimate their bodies.[46] Among the Fijians, 'when any one faints or dies, their spirit, it is said, may sometimes be brought back by calling after it; and occasionally the ludicrous scene is witnessed of a stout man lying at full length, and bawling out lustily for the return of his own soul.'[47] To the negroes of North Guinea, derangement or dotage is caused by the patient being prematurely deserted by his soul, sleep being a more temporary withdrawal.[48] Thus, in various countries, the bringing back of lost souls becomes a regular part of the sorcerer's or priest's profession. The Salish Indians of Oregon regard the spirit as distinct from the vital principle, and capable of quitting the body for a short time without the patient being conscious of its absence; but to avoid fatal consequences it must be restored as soon as possible, and accordingly the medicine-man in solemn form replaces it down through the patient's head.[49] The Turanian or Tatar races of Northern Asia strongly hold the theory of the soul's departure in disease, and among the Buddhist tribes the Lamas carry out the ceremony of soul-restoration in most elaborate form. When a man has been robbed by a demon of his rational soul, and has only his animal soul left, his senses and memory grow weak and he falls into a dismal state. Then the Lama undertakes to cure him, and with quaint rites exorcises the evil demon. But if this fails, then it is the patient's soul itself that cannot or will not find its way back. So the sick man is laid out in his best attire and surrounded with his most attractive possessions, the friends and relatives go thrice round the dwelling, affectionately calling back the soul by name, while as a further inducement the Lama reads from his book descriptions of the pains of hell, and the dangers incurred by a soul which wilfully abandons its body, and then at last the whole assembly declare with one voice that the wandering spirit has returned and the patient will recover.[50] The Karens of Burma will run about pretending to catch a sick man's wandering soul, or as they say with the Greeks and Slavs, his 'butterfly' (leip-pya), and at last drop it down upon his head. The Karen doctrine of the 'là' is indeed a perfect and well-marked vitalistic system. This là, soul, ghost, or genius, may be separated from the body it belongs to, and it is a matter of the deepest interest to the Karen to keep his là with him, by calling it, making offerings of food to it, and so forth. It is especially when the body is asleep, that the soul goes out and wanders; if it is detained beyond a certain time, disease ensues, and if permanently, then its owner dies. When the 'wee' or spirit-doctor is employed to call back the departed shade or life of a Karen, if he cannot recover it from the region of the dead, he will sometimes take the shade of a living man and transfer it to the dead, while its proper owner, whose soul has ventured out in a dream, sickens and dies. Or when a Karen becomes sick, languid and pining from his là having left him, his friends will perform a ceremony with a garment of the invalid's and a fowl which is cooked and offered with rice, invoking the spirit with formal prayers to come back to the patient.[51] This ceremony is perhaps ethnologically connected, though it is not easy to say by what manner of diffusion or when, with a rite still practised in China. When a Chinese is at the point of death, and his soul is supposed to be already out of his body, a relative may be seen holding up the patient's coat on a long bamboo, to which a white cock is often fastened, while a Taoist priest by incantations brings the departed spirit into the coat, in order to put it back into the sick man. If the bamboo after a time turns round slowly in the holder's hands, this shows that the spirit is inside the garment.[52]

Such temporary exit of the soul has a worldwide application to the proceedings of the sorcerer, priest, or seer himself. He professes to send forth his spirit on distant journeys, and probably often believes his soul released for a time from its bodily prison, as in the case of that remarkable dreamer and visionary Jerome Cardan, who describes himself as having the faculty of passing out of his senses as into ecstasy whenever he will, feeling when he goes into this state a sort of separation near the heart as if his soul were departing, this state beginning from his brain and passing down his spine, and he then feeling only that he is out of himself.[53] Thus the Australian native doctor is alleged to obtain his initiation by visiting the world of spirits in a trance of two or three days' duration;[54] the Khond priest authenticates his claim to office by remaining from one to fourteen days in a languid and dreamy state, caused by one of his souls being away in the divine presence;[55] the Greenland angekok's soul goes forth from his body to fetch his familiar demon;[56] the Turanian shaman lies in lethargy while his soul departs to bring hidden wisdom from the land of spirits.[57] The literature of more progressive races supplies similar accounts. A characteristic story from old Scandinavia is that of the Norse chief Ingimund, who shut up three Finns in a hut for three nights, that they might visit Iceland and inform him of the lie of the country where he was to settle; their bodies became rigid, they sent their souls on the errand, and awakening after the three days they gave a description of the Vatnsdæl.[58] The typical classic case is the story of Hermotimos, whose prophetic soul went out from time to time to visit distant regions, till at last his wife burnt the lifeless body on the funeral pile, and when the poor soul came back, there was no longer a dwelling for it to animate.[59] A group of the legendary visits to the spirit-world, which will be described in the next chapter, belong to this class. A typical spiritualistic instance may be quoted from Jung-Stilling, who says that examples have come to his knowledge of sick persons who, longing to see absent friends, have fallen into a swoon during which they have appeared to the distant objects of their affection.[60] As an illustration from our own folklore, the well-known superstition may serve, that fasting watchers on St John's Eve may see the apparitions of those doomed to die during the year come with the clergyman to the church door and knock; these apparitions are spirits who come forth from their bodies, for the minister has been noticed to be much troubled in his sleep while his phantom was thus engaged, and when one of a party of watchers fell into a sound sleep and could not be roused, the others saw his apparition knock at the church door.[61] Modern Europe has indeed kept closely enough to the lines of early philosophy, for such ideas to have little strangeness to our own time. Language preserves record of them in such expressions as 'out of oneself,' 'beside oneself,' 'in an ecstasy,' and he who says that his spirit goes forth to meet a friend, can still realise in the phrase a meaning deeper than metaphor.

Synkrētic

Notes

1 J. D. Lang, 'Queensland,' pp. 340, 374, 380, 388, 444 (Buddai appears, p. 379, as causing a deluge; he is probably identical with Budyah).

2 Moffat, 'South Africa,' p. 261.

3 Azara, 'Voy. Dans l'Amérique Méridionale,' vol. ii, pp. 3, 14, 25, 51, 60, 91, 119, etc. ; D'Orbigny, 'L'Homme Américain,' vol. ii, p. 318.

4 Muir, 'Sanskrit Texts,' part ii. p. 435 ; Euseb. 'Hist. Eccl.' Iv. 15 ; Bingham, book i. ch. Ii; Vanini, 'De Admirandi Naturae Arcanis,' dial. 37; Lecky, 'Hist. of Rationalism,' vol. i. p. 126 ; Encylcop. Brit. (5th ed.) s. v. 'Superstition.'

5 J. de Verrazano in Hakluyt, vol. iiii p. 300.

6 See W. Ellis, 'Hist. of Madagascar,' vol. i p. 429; Flacourt, 'Hist. de Madagascar,' p. 59.

7 Dampier, 'Voyages,' vol. ii. part ii. p. 76.

8 *Synkrētic* - The term 'Hottentot' is a now deprecated term used in the 19th century to refer to the Khoekhoe peoples of South Africa. Use of the term in this sense today is considered offensive.

9 Roe in Pinkerton, vol. viii. p. 2

10 Lubbock, 'Prehistoric Times,' p. 564: see also 'Origin of Civilization,' p. 138.

11 *Synkrētic* - The term 'Ahts' referred to one of the indigenous peoples of the Pacific Northwest Coast in Canada with traditional lands on Vancouver (formerly Quadra's and Vancouver's) Island. This people is today known as the Nuu-chah-nulth.

12 Sproat, 'Scenes and Studies of Savage Life,' p. 205.

13 Mouat, 'Andaman Islanders,' pp. 2, 279, 393. Since the above was written, the remarkable Andaman religion has been described by Mr E. H. Man, in 'Journ. Anthrop. Inst.' Vol. xii (1883), p. 156. [Note to 3rd ed.]

14 Baker, 'Races of the Nile Basin,' in Tr. Eth. Soc. Vol. v. p. 231; 'The Albert Nyanta,' vol. i. p. 246. See Kaufmann, 'Schilderungen aus Central-afrika,' p. 123; Brun-Rollet, ‚Le Nil Blanc et le Soudan,' pp. 100, 222, also pp. 164, 200, 234; G. Lejean in 'Rev. des Deux M.' April 1, 1862, p. 760; Waitz, 'Anthropologie,' vol. ii. pp. 72-6; Bastian, 'Mensch,' vol. iii. p. 298. Other recorded cases of denial of religion of savage tribes on narrow definition or inadequate evidence may be found in Meiners, 'Gesch. Der Rel.' vol. i. pp. 11-15 (Australians and Californians); Waitz, 'Anthropologie,' vol. i. p. 323 (Aru Islanders, etc.); Farrar in 'Anthrop. Rev.' Aug. 1864, p. ccxvii. (Kafirs, etc.); Martius, 'Ethnog. Amer.' vol. i. p. 58 (Manaos); J. G. Palfrey, 'Hist. of New England,' vol. i. p. 46 (New England tribes).

15 The term has been especially used to denote the doctrine of Stahl, the promulgator also of the phlogiston-theory. The Animism of Stahl is a revival and development in modern scientific shape of the classic theory identifyin vital principle and soul. See his 'Theoria Medica Vera,' Halle, 1737; and the critical dissertation on his views, Lemoine, 'Le Vitalism et l'Animisme de Stahl,' Paris, 1864.

16 Bonwick, 'Tasmanians,' p. 182.

17 Tanner's 'Narr.' p. 281, Cree atchâk = soul.
18 Brasseur, 'Langue Quichée,' s.v.
19 Martius, 'Ethnog. Amer.' vol. i. p. 705; vol. ii. p. 310.
20 Dobrizhoffer, 'Abipones,' vol. ii p. 194.
21 Döhne, 'Zulu Dic.' s.v. 'tunzi;' Callaway, 'Rel. of Amazulu,' pp. 91, 126; 'Zulu Tales,' vol. i. p. 342.
22 Casalis, 'Basutos,' p. 245; Arbousset and Daumas, 'Voyage,' p. 12.
23 Goldie, 'Efik Dictionary,' s.v.; see Kölle, 'Afr. Native Lit.' p. 324 (anuri). Also 'Journ. Ind. Achip.' Vol. v. p. 713 (Australian).
24 Dante, 'Div. Comm. Purgatorio,' canto iii. Compare Grohmann, 'Aberglauben aus Böhmen,' p. 221. See *ante*, p. 85.
25 Rochefort, pp. 429, 516; J. G. Müller, p. 207.
26 Mariner, 'Tonga Is.' vol. ii. p. 135; S. S. Farmer, 'Tonga,' etc. p. 131.
27 Casalis, l.c. See also Mariner, ibid.
28 Bastian, 'Pyschologie,' pp. 15-23.
29 J. H. Bernau, 'Brit. Guiana,' p. 134.
30 Grimm, 'D. M.' pp. 1028, 1133. Anglo-Saxon *man-lica*.
31 Lieber, 'Laura Bridgman,' in Smithsonian Contrib. vol. ii. p. 8.
32 G. F. Moore, 'Vocab. of W. Australia,' p. 103.
33 Brinton, p. 50, see p. 235; Bastian, 'Psychologie,' p. 15.
34 Cranz, 'Grönland,' p. 257.
35 Crawfurd, 'Malay Gr. and Dic.' s.v.; Marsden, 'Sumatra,' p. 386.
36 Oviedo, 'Hist. du Nicaragua,' pp. 21-51.
37 Pott, 'Zigeuner,' vol. ii. p. 306; 'Indo-Germ. Wurzel-Wörterbuch, vol. i. p. 1073; Borrow, 'Lavengro,' vol. ii. ch. xxvi. 'write the lil of him whose *dook* gallops down that hill every night,' see vol. iii. ch. iv.
38 Brinton, 'Myths of New World,' p. 253; Comm. In Virg. Æn. iv. 684; Cic. Verr. v. 45; Wuttke, ,Volksaberglaube,' p. 210; Rochholz, 'Deutscher Glaube,' etc. vol. i. p. 111.
39 Williams, 'Fiji,' vol. i. p. 241.
40 Ellis, 'Madagascar,' vol. i. p. 393.
41 Charlevoix, 'Nouvelle France,' vol. vi. pp. 75-8 ; Schoolcraft, 'Indian Tribes,' part i. pp. 33, 83, part iv. p. 70 ; Waitz, vol. iii. p. 194 ; J. G. Müller, pp. 66, 207-8.
42 Cross in 'Journ. Amer. Oriental Soc.' Vol. iv. p. 310.
43 Macpherson, pp. 91-2. See also Klemm, 'C. G.' vol. iii. p. 71 (Lapp); St John, 'Far East,' vol. i. p. 189 (Dayaks).
44 *Synkrētic* – The English translation has been taken from John Mason Good's notes to his translation of *The Nature of Things: A Didactic Poem* by Titus Lucretius Carus. See *The Nature of Things: A Didactic Poem translated from the Latin of Titus Lucretius Carus* (London: Longman, Hurst, Reese, and Orme, 1805), vol. i, p. 37.

Synkrētic

45 Shürmann, 'Vocab. of Parnkalla Lang.' s.v.
46 Tanner's 'Narr.' p. 291; Keating, 'Narr. Of Long's Exp.' vol. ii p. 154.
47 Williams, 'Fiji,' vol. i. p. 242; see the converse process of catching away a man's soul, causing him to pine and die, p. 250.
48 J. L. Wilson, 'W. Afr.' p. 220.
49 Bastian, 'Mensch,' vol. ii. p. 319; also Sproat, p. 213 (Vancouver's I.).
50 Bastian, 'Pyschologie,' p. 34; Gmelin, 'Reisen durch Sibirien,' vol. ii. p. 359 (Yakuts); Ravenstein, 'Amur,' p. 351 (Tunguz).
51 Bastian, 'Oestl. Asien,' vol. i. p. 143; vol. ii. pp. 388, 418; vol. iii. p. 236. Mason, 'Karens,' l.c. p. 196, etc.; Cross, 'Karens,' in 'Journ. Amer. Oriental Soc.' vol. iv. 1854, p. 307. See also St John, 'Far East,' l.c. (Dayaks).
52 Doolittle, 'Chinese,' vol. i. p. 150.
53 Cardan, 'De Varietate Rerum,' Basel, 1556, cap. xliii.
54 Stanbridge, 'Abor. Of Victoria,' in 'Tr. Eth. Soc.' Vol. i. p. 300.
55 Macpherson, 'India,' p. 103.
56 Cranz, 'Grönland,' p. 269. See also Sproat, l.c.
57 Rühs, 'Finland,' p. 303; Castrén, 'Finn. Myth.' p. 134; Bastian, 'Mensch,' vol. ii. p. 319.
58 Vatnsdæla Saga; Baring-Gould, 'Werewolves,' p. 29.
59 Plin. vii. 53; Lucian. Hermotimus, Musc. Encoun. 7.
60 R. D. Owen, 'Footfalls on the Boundary of another World,' p. 259. See A. R. Wallace, 'Scientific Aspect of the Supernatural,' p. 43.
61 Brand, 'Pop. Ant.' vol. i. p. 331, vol. iii. p. 236. See Calmet, 'Diss. sur les Esprits;' Maury, 'Magie,' part ii. ch. iv.

The life and writings of Avyar*

Reverend Dr John

The Malabars, or more properly the Tamils, boast of having produced the celebrated Avyar, one of their ancient moral philosophers.

This Lady's writings contain good general ideas grounded in the science of morality.

She was a polytheist, and invokes the God Suppiramanien, or Pulleyar, the Son of Siven, who is held by the Hindus to be the protector of Learning and Science, as Mercury was amongst the Greeks.

Her origin and birth, as well as the era in which she flourished, are lost in fable.

Some pretend she was a goddess, one of Brimha's wives, and had been guilty of a trespass, for which she had been driven from heaven to earth, where she was condemned to remain till she had performed sufficient atonement for her sin, by severe and long repentance. On earth she composed her moral writings, for the benefit of mankind, and particularly for youth. On account of her divine origin, she is therefore highly respected.

Others take her to be one of the seven wise or moral philosophers, in whom the Tamils glory as well as the ancient Greeks, and

---

* Republished, without annotations, from the journal *Asiatic Researches; or, Transactions of the Society instituted in Bengal, for inquiring into the History and Antiquities, the Arts, Sciences, and Literature of Asia*, Vol. 7 (1803): 343-61. This work is in the public domain.

with more reason, as they have four ladies in the number, and only three men. Their wonderful birth is related in the *Kandapranam*, of which I will give only a short extract.

The female philosophers are Avyar, Uppay, Vallie and Uruvay; and the male, the famous Tiruvalluwer (whose writings contain good and elegant moral verses) Adigaman and Kavviler.

All these seven wise persons belonged to the same family, were of the same parents, but were educated by different charitable guardians. One in the royal palace by a king, the other in the hut of a basketmaker, another by a Brahmin, another even by an outcast, and so forth, but at last they all turned out sages; their birth was not less wonderful. Their father was Perali, and their grandfather Vedamoli, both great saints and philosophers. The latter saw, once in the night, a bright star falling down, in a village inhabited by outcasts, upon a house, wherein a girl was just born. By his prophetic power, he discovered that this girl would be one day married to his son Perali, who was then a boy of twelve years of age, which made him very uneasy.

He communicated his sorrow to his fellow Brahmins, but in general terms only; he told them, that the girl born last night in the village of outcasts, under such wonderful circumstances, would entail numberless misfortunes on the Brahmin cast in general; but he carefully concealed whatever had relation to his own son, since its disclosure would have excluded him from the cast.

They were all struck with terror at this sad prophecy, and they deliberated as to the disposal of the infant. The father was called, and informed of the unlucky destiny interwoven with his child, and he was asked which ought to suffer? his child, or the revered cast of Brahmins? The poor man answered very submissively; I deliver up my child entirely to you; do with her what you think proper. The child was brought, and her death was unanimously agreed upon. Vedamoli alone withheld his consent from this barbarous decree, and, instead of the death of the child, proposed its removal to a distant place, where it might be left to its fate.

They listened to this advice, made a box, laid the child in, and put it in the holy river Kaveri, leaving it to the destiny of the Deity. During this transaction, the old prophet ordered his son to go and look at the child before it was committed to the water, and see if he could discover any distinguished mark on her body. This he did, and returned with the answer, that the child had a very distinct black mark on her thigh. The matter was now dropped, and the old man died soon after, without further explanation on the subject.

When the poor little Nayad was thus floating to a remote country, a Brahmin was on a morning at the river, washing and performing his usual devotions and ceremonies. He saw the box coming on, and instead of finding a treasure, which he expected, discovered in it a new-born smiling girl. Having no children, though he had often prayed to obtain that blessing, he imagined his Deity had heard his prayers, and favoured him with this child. He put her to nurse, and provided for her education as his own daughter. Meanwhile young Perali, having been well-instructed in philosophy, began, after the example of his late father, to travel as a Njani to visit holy places, and to converse with saints and philosophers for his improvement.

On these travels, he came accidentally to the house of that Brahmin who had adopted the girl. The Brahmin, finding him to be a fine well-informed youth, grew fond of his character and zeal in learning, kept him several years in his house, and at last married him to the girl, who generally was supposed to be his own daughter. After they had lived happy together for a while, she once returned from her oblations, and on her changing her clothes, he was thunderstruck as it were at observing the mark on her thigh, and which discovered her low birth, of which she herself was ignorant. He hid from her his anxiety, but made inquiries at other Brahmins, how his father-in-law had got this supposed daughter, and the whole secret was now disclosed to him.

Not choosing to quarrel with his father-in-law, or to appear ungrateful for the kindness and benefits which had been conferred, he was silent; but in a state of much distraction, he went away without taking leave, or saying anything either to his father-in-law or to his wife. Both were much alarmed, and the father-in-law thinking his daughter had offended her husband, or was in some way the cause of his displeasure, ordered her to go after him, and either to reconcile and bring him back, or to follow him everywhere and stay with him. She obeyed, went after him, and used every possible means to persuade him to forgive her if she had offended him, and to be cheerful and return to his father's house. But he was immoveable, answered not a single word, looked much confused, went on hastily, and endeavoured to escape from her sight. However, she followed him wherever he went, and stayed at every choultry and shettrum,[1] where he passed the night, hoping that he at last would be prevailed upon to return with her. This continued for five days, and he tired of her entreaties, in the night, watched when she fell asleep, and then he arose, left her and went away. When she awoke, she looked about, and observed with the greatest concern he was gone, and she herself quite deserted. She did not know what to do, and whither to go, nor did she venture to return to her father, whose order she wished strictly to obey, and who might perhaps think she had killed her husband when she came back without him. In this deplorable situation, she wandered about in a neighbouring village, sighing and weeping; this was observed by a Brahmin, who asked her the cause of her tears. She informed him of her sad misfortunes, and all the circumstances of her former life, so far as she herself knew them. At this he was greatly affected, bid her come to his house, and promised to take care of her as one of his own daughters. She came, and behaved in such a manner that she endeared herself to him and to all his other daughters, who treated her as a sister. When this good man died, he divided his great estate in equal portions, and she got so much that she built a shettrum, wherein she passed her days religiously, and charitably treated the pilgrims and religious travellers who came to lodge there by night, with milk, rice, fruits, and all the victuals she could afford. At the same time she endeavoured to improve by them in knowledge and virtue, asked their advice, requested them to relate to her the circumstances of their lives; and did the same respecting her own life and adventures, her object in this being to pass the time in a mutually agreeable and useful manner. When she had continued so for several years, it happened that her husband came as a pilgrim to the same shettrum, and was entertained by her in the same kind manner with which she received and entertained the other travellers. Neither knew the other. When she related also to him her adventures, he was surprised to find his wife in this virtuous person, and that he himself had so great a share in what she related. He admired her virtue and faithfulness, but was greatly confused in his mind, feigning to fall asleep during her discourse, but passed the night in the utmost anxiety. Before sunrise he arose, took his stick and little bundle, and went off without saying a word. At this she was highly surprised and affected, thinking she might have perhaps offended him, or not attended him well enough, and went therefore after him, asking, "Why do you go away so silent and troubled in mind? Have you taken perhaps any offence at me, or do you suspect my virtue? Tell and forgive, if I have done any thing amiss unknowingly. You go away just in the same manner as my husband when he left me." At this he could no longer refrain himself, he threw down his earthen vessels and bundle, and exclaimed, "Yes, I am thy husband! And thou art my wife. I have not left thee for any fault on thy side, but only for religious purposes. As thou hast remained so religious and faithful, I receive thee again, if thou wilt strictly do all that I shall order thee." Surprised and rejoiced at this happy discovery, she promised him solemnly to pay him the strictest obedience. From this time he carried her with him on all his travels, and had seven children by her, who became the abovementioned philosophers. This was indeed no great wonder, as they were born with the gifts of speech and of wisdom. She was ordered by her husband to expose the children in the woods in the open air, leaving them to Providence, without nursing, or taking any farther care of the newborn infants. This she obeyed implicitly, according to her solemn engagement, which she kept sacredly, though with inward reluctance, and the tender feelings of a mother. When she kissed and took leave of them, each began to speak and to comfort her. One said to her: 'The Deity has formed me in thy woinb, nourished me, and let me grow in it wonderfully till my birth. Dost thou now doubt that he will not provide for me further? Go, put thy trust in him, and follow his ways.' The second child said at her departure: 'God

Synkrētic

provides even for the frog in a stone, shall he do less for me? Why art thou anxious for me ? Be comforted and go.' The third replied to her: 'God has brought me into the world, and determined my fate—is he perhaps dead? He surely will not let me starve—go, dear mother, and fear nothing for my sake.' The fourth said: 'Is not the egg surrounded with a hard shell? And God notwithstanding vivifies the little brood in it—will not he feed it after it has broken through the shell? Thus he will also feed me, do not be troubled but cheerful, and be confident in his Providence.' The fifth said to her: 'He who has made the finest veins and channels within the plants, in which the nourishing particles of the earth rise and cause their growth, and who has formed the smallest insects so wonderfully in their parts, and gives them food, will not he do the same for me? Be not therefore cast down, but be in good spirits and hope in him.' The sixth said: 'Manifold and trifling are the occupations of men, but the great work of the Almighty is to create and to preserve; believe this and comfort thyself.' The seventh addressed her thus: 'God creates such different qualities in the trees and plants, that they produce sour, sweet, bitter, and various delicious fruits. He, who is powerful to do this, will also provide for me. Why dost thou weep, my dear mother? Be cheerful and hope in him.' Each of these children was soon after found, taken up, nursed, and provided for by people of the highest, middle, and lowest ranks. One by a king, another by a washerman, another by a poet and philosopher, another by a toddyman,[2] another by a basket-maker, another by a brahmin, and another by an outcast. Avyar, of whose writings I shall give some account, had the fate to be educated by the poet. The time in which she lived, is placed in the age when the three famous kings, Smolen, Sheron, and Pandiek lived, which falls about the 9th century of the Christian era.

Amongst other sciences, she was well acquainted with chemistry, and became an adept, possessing the power of making gold, the best medicine, and the famous calpam, which preserves life to a great age, and by the virtue of which she lived 240 years. From this fabulous narration, which is differently represented in several Tamil ancient writings, I will proceed to her performances, which are the little moral treatises *Atisūdi, Konnewenden, Mudurci, Nadwăli,* and *Kalvi-oluckam.* These are introduced in the Tamil schools, and read by the children amongst the first books which they learn to read. But neither the children understand it, nor can hardly any master comprehend each of the sentences they contain, as some are composed of such high and abstruse words, which admit more than one sense, and some say that each sentence could be interpreted in five different ways. Some appear to me clear enough, and admitting only one interpretation; but some are so dark, and those with whom I have consulted, vary so much amongst themselves, that I found it difficult to decide between their interpretations, and I choose therefore that which gave the best sense, and according to that manuscript which I possess, for there are also different manuscripts.

The sentences are placed according to the order of the Tamil alphabet; each accordingly begins with a letter, therefore we may call it, The Golden Alphabet of the Tamils.

I shall now give first a translation of the *Atisūdi,* and shall continue to translate the rest, if this meets with a favourable acceptance from the friends of ancient Indian learning.

Translation of the *Atisūdi* by Avyar

Glory and Honour be to the divine son of him, who is crowned with the flowers of the Ati (Bauhiuia tomentosa.)

Charity be thy pleasure.

Be not passionate.

Be not a miser in giving.

Hinder none in charity.

Do not manifest thy secrets.

Lose not thy courage.

Exercise thyself in cyphering and writing.

Synkrētic

To live on alms is shameful.
Give, and then eat.
Converse only with the peaceful.
Never cease to improve in learning.
Do not speak what is dishonest.
Do not raise the price of victuals.
Do not say more than thou hast seen.
Take care of what is most dear.
Bathe on each Saturday.
Speak what is agreeable.
Build not too large a house.
Know first one's character before thou art confident.
Honour thy father and mother.
Do not forget benefits received.
Sow in due time.
Tillage gives the best livelihood.
Do not walk about melancholy.
Do not play with snakes.
Bed thyself on cotton, (soft.)
Do not speak craftily.
Do not flatter.
Learn whilst thou art young.
Do not forget what is best for thy body.
Avoid affectation.
Forget offence.
To protect is noble.

The life and writings of Avyar

Seek a constant happiness.
Avoid what is low.
Keep strongly what is good.
Do not part with thy friend.
Do not hurt any body.
Hear and improve.
Do not use thy hands to do mischief.
Do not desire stolen goods.
Be not slothful in thy actions.
Keep strictly to the laws of the country.
Keep company with the virtuous.
Be not a scoffer.
Do not act against the custom of the country.
Make not others blush by thy speaking.
Do not love gaming.
What thou dost, do with propriety.
Consider the place where thou goest.
Do not walk about as a spy.
Do not speak too much.
Do not walk about like a dreamer.
Converse with those who are polite.
Endeavour to be settled at a fixed place.
Dedicate thyself to Tirumal, Vishtnoo.
Abhor what is bad.
Indulge not thy distress.
Save rather than destroy.

Synkrētic

Speak not disrespectfully of the Deity.
Be on good terms with thy fellow citizens.
Do not mind what women say.
Do not despise thy ancestors.
Do not pursue a conquered enemy.
Be constant in virtue.
Have a regard for country people.
Remain in thy station.
Do not play in water.
Do not occupy thyself with trifles.
Keep the divine laws.
Cultivate what gives the best fruit.
Remain constantly in what is just.
Do thy business without murmur.
Do not speak ill of any body.
Do not make thyself sick.
Mock not those who have any bodily defect.
Go not where a snake may lie.
Do not speak of others' faults.
Keep far from infection.
Endeavour to get a good name.
Seek thy livelihood by tilling the ground.
Endeavour to get the protection of the great.
Avoid being simple.
Converse not with the wicked.
Be prudent in applying thy money.

Come not near to thine adversary.

Choose what is the best.

Do not come near one who is in a passion.

Avoid the company of choleric men.

Converse with those who are meek.

Follow the advices of wise men.

Go not into the house of the dancing girls.

Speak distinctly to be well understood.

Abhor bad lusts.

Do not speak falsely.

Do not like dispute.

Love learning.

Endeavour to get a house of your own.

Be an honest man.

Live peaceful with thy fellow citizen.

Do not speak frightfully.

Do not evil purposely.

Be clean in thy clothes.

Go only where there is peace.

Love religious meditation.

End of the moral sentences given by Avyar.

Translation of the *Kalwioluckam*,[3] or *Rules of Learning* by Avyar.

The zealous study of sciences brings increasing happiness and honour.

Synkrētic

From the fifth year of age learning must begin.

The more we learn the more understanding we get.

Spare no expense to learn reading and writing.

Of all treasures, reading and writing are the most valuable.

Learning is really the most durable treasure.

An ignorant man ought to remain dumb.

He who is ignorant of reading and writing, is indeed very poor.

Though thou should'st be very poor, learn at least something.

Of each matter endeavour to get a clear knowledge.

The true end of knowledge is to distinguish good and bad.

He who has learned nothing is a confused prattler.

The five syllables Na ma si va yah contain a great mystery.

He who is without knowledge is like a blind man.

Cyphering must be learned in youth.

Be not the cause of shame to thy relations.

Fly from all that is low.

One accomplished philosopher is hardly to be met with among thousands.

A wise man will never cease to learn.

If all should be lost, what we have learned will never be lost.

He who loves instruction will never perish.

A wise man is like a supporting hand.

He who has attained learning by free self application, excels other philosophers.

Continue always in learning, though thou should'st do it at a great expense.

Enjoy always the company of wise men.

The life and writings of Avyar

He who has learned most is most worthy of honour.

What we have learned in youth, is like a writing cut in stone.

Speak the Tamil language not only elegantly, but also distinctly.

False speaking causes infinite quarrels.

He who studies sophistry and deceit, turns out a wicked man.

Science is an ornament wherever we come.

He who converses with the wicked, perishes with them.

Honour a moral master (tutor.)

Speak slowly when thou conversest or teachest.

He who knoweth himself is the wisest.

What thou hast learned teach also to others.

Learn in a proper manner, then thou wilt succeed in being wise.

He, who will be a tutor, must first have a well grounded knowledge.

If one knows what sin is, he becomes wise.

The wicked will not accept of instruction.

Do not fix thy attention on vain women.

Well principled wise men approach the perfection of the Divinity.

Begin thy learning in the name of the Divine Son, (Pulleyar.)

Endeavour to be respected amongst men by learning.

Let thy learning be thy best friend.

Use the strongest entreaties where thou canst learn something, then wilt thou become a great man in the world.

All perishes except learning.

Though one is of a low birth, learning will make him respected: Religious wise men enjoy great happiness.

Though thou should'st be one hundred years old, endeavour still to increase in knowledge.

Synkrētic

Wisdom is firm grounded even on the great ocean.
Without wisdom, nowhere is there ground to stand upon.
Learning also suits old age.
Wise men will never offend any by speaking.
Accept instructions even from men of a low birth.
Do not behave impolitely to men of learning.
Poets require a great deal of learning.
The unwise only flatter others.
Seek honor, and thou shalt get it.
The virtuous are also tutors.
Wisdom is the greatest treasure on earth.
The wiser the more respected.
Learning gives great fame.
Learn one thing after the other, but not hastily.
A science in which we take no pleasure is like a bitter medicine.
Speak so that town and country people may understand thee.
Wise men are as good as kings.
Do not deceive even thine own enemy.
Hast thou learned much, communicate it also in an agreeable manner.
In whom is much science, in him is great value.
The present Tamil language does not equal the old.
He that knows the sciences of the ancients is the greatest philosopher.
Truth is in learning the best.
Wise men are exalted above all other men.
True philosophy does not suffer a man to be put in confusion.

In proportion as one increases in learning, he ought also to increase in virtue.

The most prosperous good is the increase in learning.

He who has no knowledge knows not also the truth.

Wisdom is a treasure valued everywhere.

A good tutor is beloved over the whole world.

What we gain by science is the best estate, (inheritance).

Adore the Goddess Sarasbadi.

The *Vedam* (sacred writings) teaches wisdom.

Speak and write for the benefit of the public.

He who speaks well and connectedly, is best understood by all.

If knowledge has a proper influence on the mind, it makes us virtuous.

End of the moral book Kalwioluckam, *composed by* Avyar.

Translation of the small Tamil book *Konneivenden*,[4] written by the female philosopher Avyar

Continual praise be to the Son of him, who is crowned with the flower of Konnei (Poinciana pulcherrima.)

Mother and Father are the first known Deity.

A good man attendeth religious service.

Without one's own house there is nowhere a good lodging.

The estate of the wicked will be robbed by the wicked.

Modesty is the best ornament of the fair sex.

If one maketh himself hateful to his fellow creatures, he must entirely perish.

Exercise in writing and cyphering is most useful.

Synkrētic

Obstinate children are like a poisonous draft.
Though thou art very poor, do what is honest.
Adhere chiefly to the only one constantly.
The virtuous will always improve in wisdom and knowledge.
A wicked mouth destroys all wealth.
Seek wealth and money, but without quarrel.
Give in writing what shall stand fast.
A woman must attend herself best.
Even with thy nearest friends speak not impolitely.
Speak friendly even to the poor.
If one will criticise, he will find some fault everywhere.
Speak not haughtily, though thou art a great man.
To pardon is better than to revenge.
What shall stand firm must have witnesses.
Wisdom is of greater value than ready money.
To be on good terms with the King is useful in due time.
A calumnious mouth is a fire in the wood.
Good advisers are hated by the world.
The best ornament of a family is unanimity.
What a senior says, must a junior not despise.
If thou cherishest passion, all thy merit is lost.
Get first the plough, and then look out for the oxen.
A moral life has a happy influence on the public.
Gaming and quarrelling bring misery.
Without practical virtue there is no merit.
Keep a proper time even for thy bed.

Be peaceful, give and be happy.

A merchant must be careful with money.

Laziness brings great distress.

To obey the father is better than prayer.

To honour the mother is better than divine service.

Seek thy convenient livelihood shouldst thou even do it upon the sea.

Irreconcileableness ends in quarrel.

A bad wife is like a fire in the lap.

A slandering wife is like a devil.

Without the mercy of the Deity nothing will prosper.

He who squanders away even what he has not gained justly must perish at last.

In January and February sleep under a good roof.

Better eat by hard labour than by humble begging.

Speak not what is low even to thy friend.

Without a clean conscience there is no good sleep.

If the public is happy, all are safe.

Improvement in wisdom improves our veracity.

Seek a house where good water is at hand.

Deliberate first well what thou art going to begin.

The reading of good books will improve welfare.

Who speaks as he thinks is an upright man.

What we propose we must pursue with zeal.

We must not speak dishonestly even to a poor man.

Dishonesty will end in infamy.

Laziness brings lamentations.

Synkrētic

The fruit will be equal to the seed.
We cannot always drink milk but must submit to the time.
An honest man does not touch another's property.
The name of a true great man will ever remain in esteem.
Lies are as much as murder and robbery.
What honesty can be expected from low fellows?
Amongst relations civility is often neglected.
A mild temper is a beauty in women.
The meek are the happiest.
Keep thyself from all that is bad.
Wisdom is the direct way to Heaven.
Let thy fellow creatures partake in thy enjoyments.
Where there is no rain, there is no crop.
After lightning follows rain.
Without a good steerer a ship cannot sail.
Who sows in time will have a good crop.
The precepts of the old ought to be cheerfully observed.
Who keeps the proper time to sleep will sleep well.
The plough never will let one suffer want.
Live in matrimony and be moderate.
Who breaks his word loses his interest.
Abhor and fly from lasciviousness.
Gain by deceit will at last be lost.
If Heaven is not favourable nothing will prosper.
From impolite people honesty can't be expected.
The words of the haughty are like arrows.

The life and writings of Avyar

A family ought to support their poor.

A great man must also have a great mind.

A good man will never deceive.

If the Lord is angry, no man can save.

All the world shall praise God.

Sleep on a safe place.

Without religion is no virtue.

End of the moral sentences called Konneivenden, *written by* Avyar.

Notes

1 *choultry and shettrum*: refer to resting places or inns for travellers or pilgrims. Variant spellings include chottry, choultree, choutry, chatra, chatram, satram.
2 *toddyman*: refers to a person who collects and prepares toddy, the sweet white sap of various Asian and African palm trees used as a drink after rapid fermentation (palm wine).
3 *Kalwioluckam*: previously (p. 74) spelled *Kalvi-oluckam*, the inconsistency is the author's.
4 *Konneivenden*: previously (p. 74) spelled *Konnewenden*, the inconsistency is the author's.

The critique of language*

Fritz Mauthner†

TRANSLATED BY *Christian Romuss*‡

Primitive Philosophy

The beautiful sentence: *Completeness is the death of scholarship*, was arguably minted by its coiner, Wilamowitz-Moellendorf,[1] only against those professors who cannot to their satisfaction gather enough scholarly references about every trifle; in the historical sciences, however, the obsessive pursuit of history into ages of which we can know nothing continues to be inherited down the generations. This obsession has been further intensified by Darwinism or the doctrine of evolution; in earnest one set about tracing all human culture's forms of expression back to their primordial origins. Even the philosophy of primordial man, primitive philosophy, was supposed to be extrapolated; the protoplasm of philosophy was supposed to be discovered or constructed.

---

* The following extracts are from Fritz Mauthner's *Wörterbuch der Philosophie. Neue Beiträge zu einer Kritik der Sprache* (Munich: Georg Müller, 1910-1911). This work, *Dictionary of Philosophy: New Contributions to a Critique of Language*, is in the public domain in the original German and available on archive.org. It remains untranslated into English. This is the second selection of extracts to be published in *Synkrētic* (see 'The critique of language' in *Synkrētic №2*, pp. 148-152).

† Fritz Mauthner (1849-1923) was a Bohemian Jewish journalist, writer and philosopher. His best-known works are *Contributions to a Critique of Language* (1901-2), *Dictionary of Philosophy* (1910-1911) and *Atheism and its History in the West* (1920-23). He lived in Berlin, Freiburg, and Meersburg, Germany.

‡ Christian Romuss is a Brisbane-based translator. He is editor of *Synkrētic*.

The critique of language

We laugh today when we read, as a chapter-heading in Brucker's 'Brief Questions about Philosophical History from the Beginning of the World to the Birth of Christ' (1731), the question: *Were there already philosophers before the flood?* And when, in the subsequent section, we find an almost hilarious refutation of the claim that Adam was a perfect dialectician, physicist, ethicist, mathematician, politician, and finally the most perfect polyhistor. We laugh at Brucker, despite the fact that he treats the question not without some irony. Likewise, we ought not to take the latest attempts to write a history of primitive philosophy in less biblical language all too seriously.

I'm thinking in that regard of Wundt's essay 'The Origins of Philosophy and the Philosophy of the Primitive Races' (Culture of the Present, Part I, Sect. V). Wundt writes at length about primitive logic, primitive psychology, primitive natural philosophy, and primitive ethics. He espouses that dangerous principle of historical scholarship which equates, on one hand, the beginnings of a cultural domain and, on the other, the relevant circumstances of the so-called primitive races of the present day; for that reason, the concepts 'origins of philosophy' and 'philosophy of the primitive races' are for him equivalent. He sees quite well that primitive philosophy was not yet acquainted with our logic; that the doctrine of the soul of primordial ages still influences our psychology; that primitive natural philosophy to be sure already possessed the concept of cause but considered magic, the miracle-working God, a sufficient cause; that the primitive ethics of the primitive races often enough rivals the so-called illuminated ethics of our Christian and philosophical West. For comparative anthropology, such investigations may yield some godless proposition or other, which Wundt is wary of formulating explicitly.

If we wanted to deal seriously with the question about a primitive philosophy, then we would have first to define both words for this context more precisely.

Primitive is a terribly relative concept. When in art history one speaks of the primitive, then one thinks of Italian painters of the 15th century and, in turn, of English painters of the 19th; therefore of painters of a very historical period who were (or acted) only

Synkrētic

somewhat more childish and more inept than the classical masters. In geology, regarding primitive mountain ranges one thinks of a primordial age which, according to the current doctrine, preceded man's existence by hundreds of thousands of years. Otherwise, *primitive* means as much or as little as primordial, original, prehistoric, or: whatever today lives in the cultural conditions which we postulate to be the most ancient conditions of today's civilised races. Conditions, therefore, about which nothing can be discerned without that foolhardy conclusion by analogy.

Philosophy, in turn, means today approximately so much as critique of knowledge; in earlier centuries, the word meant successively one or the other yearning for knowledge: of pure reason, of the connection between spirit and body, of the divine essence, of the relation between idea and individual, and so on. Now, when good old Brucker asked who the first philosopher was, this had—according to the state of historical scholarship at that time—the sense: whether one of the philosophical schools which tradition had always recognised was to be attested or not in the pronouncements of Adam which had been handed down. If today the question is posed, whether the so-called primitive races have, whether therefore the prehistoric races had a world-view to which the current concept of philosophy could still be applied, then this does not have such a clear sense. No longer believing in Adam, we must shift the primordial age further and further into the past, and with the concept of philosophy we must carry out a change in meaning which is almost no longer permissible.

Since we have become accustomed to letting man's evolution begin with animals, we would, acting consequently, therefore also have to seek out our primitive philosophy in the soul-life of animals. And in so doing it would become apparent that we understand historical and even the most modern philosophy to be man's most conscious reflecting on the foundation of his acting and knowing; that, in contrast, we invest with a primitive philosophy also such utterances of the 'savages' of whose importance they themselves were never conscious. Even the actions and world-orientations of animals could easily be arranged according to concepts which be-

The critique of language

long to human logic, psychology, natural philosophy, and ethics; and even to the writing of a 'philosophy of animals' I raise no objection whatever—if only we do not lose the sober-mindedness which recognises that doing so involves an audacious extension of human concepts.

And unfortunately with such investigations this fact is gladly overlooked. We cannot infer the primitive philosophy, and not even the philosophy of the primitive races; we can only seek to answer the question: *What, in ancient times, was understood by the words which have directly or in translation become the technical expressions of our philosophy?* and: *In what sense do some of these expressions permit themselves to be applied to the thinking of primitive races?* In inferring a primordial philosophy, I do not believe we shall get beyond a fragmentary word-history of the general-language concepts of philosophy and an attempt, by means of a retroactive change of meaning, to extend those words to embrace the notions of ancient races and living cannibals, whatever those notions may be.

It may indeed be the case that amongst the notions of ancient races and the savage peoples of today there are some with which the word-book of our philosophy[2] is not in the least acquainted; we would then, however, be in no position at all to become acquainted with such notions, to translate them into the language of our philosophy. I confess, however, that I do not believe in the existence of arcane primitive wisdom. Much nearer to me is the sombre thought that philosophy's ultimate questions have always been posed by the frailty of human sense and of human understanding in a consistent form, that the progress of language consisted only in formulating the questions more definitely, and that we hope less today than in primordial ages to find an answer for them. In feeling this resignation, we could quite easily call our modern critique of knowledge the first, the primitive philosophy.

Religion

Clarity is harsh as moonlight on a bright winter's night. Only we want to beware of becoming unjust out of harshness, and of accus-

Synkrētic

ing of hypocrisy all those who long ago lost their belief in a beloved God yet purport to have religion or religiosity.

In that respect we are dealing with a linguistic case not altogether isolated: we possess a concept for a plurality of similar phenomena but have no notion of this concept in the singular. *Religion* encompasses, as the case may be, polytheism and monotheism or Christianity, Islam and Judaism or at once myriad confessions which, in turn, are all mere buzzwords for a mélange of ritual acts, tenets, and moral conventions; this generic concept *religion* can be well or poorly defined. Now, good men, having shed the belief in God and the connection with a particular confession, believe they can also apply this content-poor generic concept to the feeling which remains with them in confronting the world-whole. It is considered indecent not to have even a skerrick of religion left over; it is said in praise of Spinoza and Goethe that theirs were deeply religious natures; and even our monists place value on designating that whereof even they know nothing as a monistic religion.

The inability to gain some notion of the singularity *religion* (if one does not by that term understand precisely the generic concept of all religions) will become clearer when I put the reader in mind of a remote concept. *Triangle* is a good generic concept for the various kinds of triangles; of a triangle, however, which is neither plane nor spherical, neither acute nor right-angled nor obtuse, I can form no notion.

Despite that, the best writers of all modern civilised nations, even after the victory of deism no longer tolerated the profession of a particular religion, continued to use the word *religion* in good conscience for man's relation to the nameless or even to the immanent God of their world-view. I merely wish to quote the two famous epigrams of Schiller and of Goethe. Schiller says:

> 'Which religion I profess? None
> of those
> which you name for me. – And why
> none? – For reason of religion.'

The ageing Goethe says:

The critique of language

'Whoever has science and art
has religion too;
whoever has neither of these,
may he have religion!'

In both instances, *religion* is set against one or the other of the organised club-religions; and approximately thus do all our liberated writers use the word 'religion' in the singular; we still pique ourselves somewhat on asserting this quite personal feeling in the face of the churches' universally binding statutes.

Now, it is however highly likely that *binding* is the original sense of Latin *religio*; Cicero's derivation from Latin *re-legere* is arguably untenable;[3] the derivation of Lactantius[4] from Latin *religare* can appeal to Aulus Gellius (IV, 9)[5] and could very well be the loan-translation of a Greek concept. However, with a word of such immesaurable historical influence it isn't really a matter of etymology and, without such help, we have only to answer two simple questions: *Does the word 'religion' still have a sense when it no longer signifies the relationship of man to a personal God?* And: *What do modern atheists believe they understand when they boast at once of their atheism and of their religious feeling?*

The first question is very difficult to answer with regard to the leading minds because we can almost never know whether they refrained from professing their atheism out of fear of the stake or, in the most recent centuries, out of the equally excusable fear of social ostracism. Compare with this the fact that two masterful texts on this topic, one from Hume and one from Schopenhauer, were written in dialogue form precisely so that the author's final view could be pinned on one of the interlocutors. Hume and Schopenhauer give for that reason no definite answer to their questions but arrive at a comfortable: yes *and* no. Schopenhauer initially wonders whether religion should be preserved for the *people*; but religion (*i.e.*, religion in the singular) also seems to him an attempt to satisfy man's metaphysical need. A hundred years prior, Hume with his *Dialogues Concerning Natural Religion* was in a more difficult situation, and arguably for that reason did not publish the delightful text during his lifetime; Schopenhauer clearly and consciously called himself an atheist, Hume only called himself a skeptic. From the historical standpoint, the book of the Scotsman is a great deal freer and more substantial than the almost political book of the German; but with regard to the questions we have posed, more important is the thought-process of the atheist, who at least under one mask advocates for religion, while under the other mask (which more closely resembles the belligerent author) he would like to eradicate religion from the earth; the Greeks, whom he deified, would not have recognised at all what we understand by the term 'religion'; even as a means of repression for the people, according to Schopenhauer, religion is only a necessary evil, the Lord God only a Knecht Ruprecht with which to chase big children to bed. Against the political maintenance of religion he quotes a sentence from Condorcet: 'toute religion, qu'on se permet de défendre comme un croyance qu'il est utile de laisser au peuple, ne peut plus espérer qu'une agonie plus ou moins prolongée.'[6] But both interlocutors are of the opinion that religion is to be regarded highly as a symbol of truth; as if any philosopher had ever been in possession of the guaranteed and certified truth.

The sublime Strauss[7] approached the question from an entirely different angle, from the standpoint of the history of theology. He wrote his confession *The Old Faith and the New* in jubilant confidence following Germany's rebirth, in the name of the *we* who had inwardly set themselves free from the old faith. Schleiermacher, a Christian hostile to dogma, had called religion a feeling (one is reminded of Jacobi), the feeling of dependency as such; Feuerbach had recognised the gods as creations of the human fancy and well saw that man would have no gods if he had no desires. What man would like to be but what he is not—for that makes he his God; what he would like to have but knows not how to procure for himself—that shall his God procure for him. Strauss, the theologian gone rogue, was all too heavily inclined towards the dogmas of materialism, just as his belief in the materialistic Darwinism of the German science of the day is the only genuine error of his confessional book. Thus, in our question too, he positioned himself decisively on the side of Feuerbach: because we can no longer believe in a personal God, we therefore no longer have religion. Religion is no advantage of human nature but a weakness inherent in the childhood of the race; the religious domain in the human soul is akin to the territory of the redskins in America, which year by year is further constrained by the civilised pale-faces. But Strauss does not stop with this rejection. Without belief in God there is properly no religion; but, for better or for worse, the word *religion* does exist and so it shall yet signify something. If we feel ourselves no longer dependent on God, then we continue to feel dependent on the universe. Strauss polemicises against Schopenhauer and claims that religion has not been extinguished within us. It still exists because it still reacts to injuries. 'When it is insulted, our feeling for the universe reacts downright religiously.' Thus he finally answers the question whether we still have religion with a snug: it depends.

I could compare yet other writers on this topic, such as Voltaire (the article 'Religion' in his *Philosophical Dictionary*), and the result would always be that these free men hated positive religion, especially the dominant Christianity; that, however, they believed it impossible to get along without the concept of religion, without a natural religion to which they gladly gave a form according to the latest philosophical systems. What we call our world-view, which of course we invest vaguely enough with some awe and some yearning too, adding to it also our mystical need, this was called by all these men: religion. I would not balk at the word although often enough there is hidden within it a cowardly compromise with church creed. It's not about the look of the word; and *religion* rolls more readily off the tongue than: feeling of yearning, feeling of awe.

All our anti-christians, from Nietzsche to Haeckel,[8] want to be founders of religion; and indeed their apostles, were it only possible, would see to it that churches were established in their names. As if we were not already dependent enough on our entire environment (on nature, to which we of course belong as a minuscule part), the yearning for a personal dependence—for a personal dependence on a supernatural being—is being expressed again more strongly in our unsatisfied age. And this yearning is so fervent that (almost as was the case with Kant) it *demands* a religious feeling from all men. So

Synkrētic

intolerant is that world-view which calls itself religious that I would like to see the concept *religion* avoided. I would not like to eradicate from the earth the religious feeling, I would only like to banish the word *religion* from clear and solid speech. There just are religious and irreligious men; there is nothing to be done about that. This relation to the concept of religion has nothing to do with the value of men. There are believing scoundrels and unbelieving mystics.

We have all passed through one or multiple forms of religion, and because of this wandering, the word-echo *religion* lingers solemnly in our hearing like the sounds of the organ and the chiming of bells. But because the word *religion*, in its long transformation of meaning, has not entirely surrendered its relationships to a personal God who through gifts and prayers can be disposed favourably toward our momentary desires; because we can hold out our little finger as little to the Church as to the Devil without fear of being eaten whole; for that reason we would do well to call our awe for life, our wistful, unobtrusive ignorance which must be deemed a world-view, religion no longer.

Notes

1 *Wilamowitz-Möllendorf*: refers to Enno Friedrich Wichard Ulrich von Wilamowitz-Moellendorff (1848-1931), a German classical philologist.

2 *word-book of our philosophy*: translates 'das Wörterbuch unserer Philosophie' = 'the dictionary of our philosophy'. I have translated *Wörterbuch* literally as word-book (strictly: words-book / book of words) to capture the analogy with such words as *Wortgeschichte* (word-history) and to preserve the concreteness of the German.

3 *Cicero's derivation*: likely refers to *De Natura Deorum* (*On the Nature of the Gods*), II, 71-72 by Roman philosopher and statesman Marcus Tullius Cicero (106-43 BC).

4 *the derivation of Lactantius*: likely refers to the *Institutiones Diviniae* (*The Divine Institutes*), IV, 28 by Lucius Caecilius Firmianus (c. 250 – c. 325), an early Christian author.

5 *can base itself on Aulus Gellius (IV, 9)*: refers to the *Noctes Atticae* (*Attic Nights*) by Roman author Aulus Gellius. Passage 9 of Book IV discusses the meaning of the term *religiosus*.

6 *a sentence from Condorcet*: refers to Marie Jean Antoine Nicolas de Caritat, Marquis of Condorcet (1743-1794), known as Nicolas de Condorcet, French political economist and mathematician. The quotation comes from Condorcet's 1795 work *Esquisse d'un*

tableau historique des progrès de l'esprit humain (*Sketch for a Historical Picture of the Progress of the Human Mind*): 'every religion which men permit themselves to defend as a creed useful to be left to the people, can expect no other fate than a dissolution more or less distant.'

7   *the sublime Strauss*: refers to David Friedrich Strauss (1808-1874), a Protestant theologian renowned for his historical investigation of Jesus. His most famous work is *Das Leben Jesu, kritisch bearbeitet* (*The Life of Jesus, Critically Examined*), published in 1835/6. His final work, *Der alte und der neue Glaube* (*The Old Faith and the New*), was published in 1872.

8   *Haeckel*: refers to Ernst Heinrich Philipp August Haeckel (1834-1919), or simply Ernst Haeckel, a German polymath known in his lifetime as the principal advocate in Germany of Charles Darwin's views on evolution.

Logomania

Ruth Aarker[*]

He talked himself
free of every counsel
which sense gave,
getting sot on the word,
a tale he told and heard
for comfort, to lave
out the spot. Doubtless
it swayed him to faith
in his own rightness.
By his reckoning:
a godwrought must –
but this, in lay ratios, just
the tongue deafening
the ear, turning sightless
the eye.

---

[*] Ruth Aarker is an Australian poet currently living in Adelaide, South Australia. *Logomania* is her first published poem.

Synkrētic
SUBMISSIONS

Australia and its place in the world continue to evolve. Now more than ever, we have to understand our region and our place in it. *Synkrētic* is an outlet for thought-provoking writing on philosophy, literature and cultures, from and about the Indo-Pacific. It aims to showcase the diverse traditions of thought, story-telling and expression which are woven into the living tapestry of this culturally, linguistically and politically complex region. We're looking above all for well-written and substantive pieces for publication in the following formats.

Essays	3000 - 6000 words
Stories	≤ 8000 words
Responses	800 - 1600 words
Translations	≤ 8000 words
Notes	300 - 3000 words

For details and guidelines:
synkretic.com

www.ingramcontent.com/pod-product-compliance
Lightning Source LLC
Chambersburg PA
CBHW022019290426
44109CB00015B/1239